NAUGHTY NOMAD'S
Guide to
NEW YORK CITY

How to get laid and party like a rock star in New York City.

Written and researched

by Mark Zolo

DEDICATION

This book is dedicated to my two younger brothers, both of whom lived with me in the city, and to my NYC wingmen, friends, and girlfriends (especially the brat who helped me with the artwork).

New York wouldn't have been the same without you guys.

High fives all 'round!

CONTENTS

ACKNOWLEDGMENTS

First, I'd like to thank my editors Matt Forney (mattforney.com) and Niall D. for helping me with the descriptive chapters of this book. I'm equally thankful to my illustrator P. Tapia, who even took off her clothes and posed for the cover. Props to Killian for his input on the typeface.

I'd also like to extend my gratitude to the NYC playboys who offered valuable insight into the city, namely Dom (dominictaurus.com), Steve (www.nycdaygame.com), and Goldmund (goldmundunleashed.com).

WELCOME TO NEW YORK CITY

"New York is the only city-city."

- Truman Capote

Growing up, New York City always seemed like the center of the universe. No other cityscape is more instantly recognizable. Iconic images like the Statue of Liberty, Central Park, the Empire State Building, and the Brooklyn Bridge are so familiar they might as well have been tattooed onto our mothers' tits. No place is featured more in popular culture either; from songs to TV shows to just about every disaster movie you've ever seen. It's the biggest city of the only superpower, the home of the United Nations, and for all intents and purposes the unofficial capital of planet Earth. For many, it's considered the greatest city of them all.

After traveling to well over 200 cities and nearly 100 countries in my lifetime, I can confirm what the hype is about. New York is, in the truest sense of the word, *awesome*. En-route home to Europe from the Caribbean, I only came to NYC for a stop-off, but became so enamored with the city that I ended up hanging out here for nearly two years. As somebody known as the "naughty nomad" who has spent his adult life banging his way across continents, that says it all.

Why New York?

In New York, it feels like you can travel the world on a metro card. This is no multicultural melting pot, but a mixed salad, a city of immigrants with a thousand tribes and languages. Everybody carves out their corner. The Greeks run the diners, the Arabs run the delis, the Irish run the bars, and you'll find restaurants with the "national cuisine" of pretty much every other country you can think of. You can't find something called Cuban cuisine in Havana, but you can be damned sure you'll find it in New York!

If you know where to look, you can pretty much get whatever you want in the. city You're spoiled for choice. One day, you could be sharing Ethiopian injera with a Korean hostess in Spanish Harlem, and the next you could joining a Jamaican stripper in a Russian Banya, and the next you're sampling Mexican mescals with an Arab student in Chinatown.

Speaking of drinking, the choice is overwhelming. There are thousands of bars and clubs. Then you've got your speakeasies, Hookah lounges, Spanish spots, underground kink parties, warehouse raves, and just about every other conceivable form of adult entertainment.

Wanna get high, too? There are street dealers in your neighbor who keep regular business hours, and if you get the late night munchies, you can be sure there's a 24-hour deli nearby with a sandwich menu so extensive it will hurt your brain.

Looking to get laid? This place is as close as you can get to pussy paradise in the first world. Women are abundant, easily available, and come in every shape and shade imaginable. Latin, Asian,

White, Black, Middle Eastern: everything is on the menu. Furthermore, women here are uninhibited, and once you crack the code, you'll get laid with minimum effort. Whether you're a complete newbie, a seasoned player, or just a regular Joe, the information I'm about to share with you will be invaluable for any guy wanting to play the game in New York City. This book will help you understand the playing field, teach you the rules, and give you the best strategies for scoring. The rest is up to you.

Why I Wrote This Book

I didn't write this book just for the money. If that were the case, it might as well carry a 'not-for-profit' label. The meager amount of income it will provide me will probably never make up for the amount of cash I've blown getting shit-faced on nights out doing so-called research. I'm ashamed to say that I've literally pissed thousands upon thousands of dollars against the wall: so much so that if all the estuaries of urine I've discharged in subway-adjacent doorways flowed into an imaginary river tomorrow, you could probably kayak to Connecticut. Add to that the cost of taxis, late-night kebabs, and the potential medical expenses from future liver damage, and I've made this book at a resounding loss.

No, *mis amigos*, I mainly wrote this book for *you*. For every horny chap who's ever had a boner, but didn't where to point it: I'm here to show you the way, my son. I wrote this guide because I wished there was somebody to show *me* the shortcuts.

And finally, I wrote this guide because I just love to write. I want to share what I've learned and contribute to a community of men who are focused on getting the most out of life. That's you fine fellows.

If you're the type of man that picks up a book in an effort to enrich your knowledge and improve your life, I tip my hat. This guide is my gift to you. I hope you get laid like a boss.

The Basics

Before you book your tickets, I'd like to offer you guys a little bit of advice: don't get your hopes up too high. The Big Apple is not something you chow down in a weekend. Most people who've been living here for years still feel like they haven't even scratched the surface of this great city. You need a week minimum to get a feel for the place. You also need to think about your budget. While you can get by surprisingly cheap in NYC, accommodation is very expensive. Things get fully booked fast too, so reserve well in advance.

WHEN TO VISIT

Like its inhabitants, New York's weather is one of extremes. If you're only coming for a short visit, I don't recommend you come around January and February because you'll freeze your balls off. Around this time of year, women go into hibernation to feast on boy-nuts and Netflix anyway. On the other end of the spectrum, the peak of summer can be uncomfortably hot and humid, reaching well into the 90s (mid-to-high 30s in Celsius). The best time of year to visit is September/October. This is when the weather is perfect. It's hot enough to wear a t-shirt during the day, but cool enough to wear a blazer at night. This is also the start of the first student semester, so the city is buzzing. Late spring to early summer is the next best option, but the weather is a lot more unpredictable, and there's not much of a student scene. There is also something undeniably magical about the city around Christmas time, but flights aren't cheap.

Pro tip: Make sure you avoid the period before and during college exams, as pussy supply decreases significantly. This is usually early-to-mid December and early to mid-May.

GETTING THERE

Use the Skyscanner app to find the cheapest deals from your country or city. If you're coming from Europe, the cheapest way to get to the east coast is via Norwegian Airlines or Icelandic WOW airlines. I was able to fly from New York to Oslo for only €129 at one point.

If you're coming from Australia or New Zealand, the cheapest way to get to the U.S. is via Jetstar to Hawaii. If you plan ahead, you can stop off there and get a cheap domestic flight to the mainland.

From Central and South America, the cheapest routes to New York are from the Caribbean Islands (especially Trinidad, Bahamas, DR, and Haiti), Mexico, Colombia, Panama, and Costa Rica. The airlines to check out are JetBlue and Spirit.

From Africa and the Middle East, Etihad, Emirates, and South African Airways usually have the best deals in most countries. Oddly enough, it is often cheaper to fly from Southern Africa than West Africa.

From Asia, the cheapest places to fly from are Seoul and Bangkok. Book at the right time and you can find flights for under $400. You can also find good deals from China and Japan.

BACHELOR'S BUDGET

Contrary to popular belief, you can get by in New York pretty cheaply, especially when it comes to eating and drinking. Happy hours, midweek dollar beer nights, and cheap grub are all easy to find. Transportation is also very reasonable. Taxis are inexpensive, and a weekly metro card with unlimited rides on both subways and buses will only set you back $31. There are other costs you may also need to consider such as tips ($1 minimum per drink), hidden sales taxes (added on top of the stated price for almost everything), and sightseeing activities ($20-30 a pop). Accommodation, however, should be the main consideration for your budget.

For those of you staying longer than a month, skip to the 'renting and long-term stay' section for a better idea of costs and other information.

Option 1: Traveling solo on the cheap

If you're traveling alone, the cheapest option would be to either use couchsurfing.org (unreliable and risky) or get a dorm bed in a hostel for $30-50 a night. If you do this, eat out at delis, pregame at home, and go out in the likes of the Lower East Side or Williamsburg, you can easily have a pretty fun time in NYC for around $80-$100 a day. If you cut out the drinking and are exceptionally frugal, you could even get by on $50 a day.

That said, I strongly recommend you *don't* get a hostel because they dramatically lower your chances of getting laid. Most hostels don't accept 'guests', and even if they did, you'd find that not every girl wants to have ninja sex in a room full of strangers. Your options are therefore limited to:

a) Picking up a girl who is staying at your hostel.

b) Finding a girl with her own place.

c) Shelling out for a cheap room at 4 a.m.

d) My personal favorite: banging a girl in the nearest bathroom.

These are all good ideas, but your best option—or at least most foolproof—is to have your *own* place to bring girls back to.

Option 2: Traveling solo in style

If you truly want the NYC bachelor experience, I recommend you budget around $150 - $200 a day. This extra cash will get you an AirBnB apartment or a basic hotel room for $80-120, and give you more play money for food and booze. The advantages of having your own room are numerous, but the main one is obvious: logistics for sexy fun time. Also, a little extra spending money will gain you access to venues with better quality women.

Option 3: Traveling with wingmen

This is the ideal scenario. If you're traveling in a group of two or more, it makes absolutely no sense to stay in a hostel. For almost the same price per person, you can share a cheap hotel room or rent an apartment. It's a no-brainer. If you split accommodation, for $100-$150 a day you'll have a place to bang, and enough cash to eat out and get you shit-faced on a pub crawl (presuming you avoid anywhere with a guest list, that is).

Option 4: Models, bottles, and lots of drugs

For those with a bit more of a bankroll, say $300-500+ a day, your options are plentiful. A mid-range hotel room in Midtown or a good apartment will set you back around $150+ a night. You'll also have enough spare cash for a plethora of narcotics, a Broadway show here or there, and a fetching hat procured whilst skipping through a night market. As for hitting high-end clubs, bottle service starts at $50-$125 per person in a decent club (although some meatpacking places typically charge $200 per person). For non-Americans, note that a sales tax will also be added to your bill and you'll also be expected to stump up a 20% gratuity on top of that.

WHERE TO STAY

Now that you have a rough idea of your budget, the next step is deciding what area of the city you want stay in. Obviously, you want to be in the thick of the action with easy access to nightlife, the sights, and multiple subway lines. If I had to recommend only one area, it would be around Union Square. Here you have seven different subway lines at one station, you're within walking distance of a ton of nightlife in East Village, and you're no more than three stops away from the action in the Lower East Side (LES), Williamsburg, Greenwich, and Times Square. You're also right by New York University (NYU), so there's plenty of talent in the area. After that, my order of preference would be as follows: Greenwich Village (east of 14th St. Station), Midtown (near any major station near Times Square, Penn Station, Herald Square, Grand Central or Lexington), the Lower East Side (near Broadway-Lafayette or Canal St. station), and Williamsburg (near the L train stops for Bedford or Metropolitan). Otherwise, pretty much anywhere on the L train line is good.

Of course, where you stay will largely depend on your budget, but hopefully you now have an idea of what areas you should be aiming for. If you're on a very tight budget and cannot afford to stay in any of the areas I've mentioned above, the best compromise would be nearby neighborhoods such as the Upper West Side, the Upper East Side and Astoria in Queens (provided you're near a subway station).

RENTING AND LONG-TERM STAYS

Prepare to be fucked in the ass. Finding a place to rent in New York City is a bitch. With the most expensive rents in the USA, prepare to pay top dollar to greedy brokers for tiny spaces in old, pre-war buildings with rats, roaches, and the occasional drive-by shooting. Okay, I'm being a little dramatic, but then again, this is a reality for some folks in the Big Rotten Apple. Finding a place to stay here can be a soul-destroying experience. Unless you're an American citizen or have already secured a high-paying job in the city, you can pretty much forget about leasing an apartment anywhere centrally located. A good credit score, proof of significant income (forty times your rent), a W2, and sometimes a guarantor are often required before you're even considered for a lease. Sure, three month's rent upfront might get you a place in Sunnyside, Queens, or Bushwick, Brooklyn, but Manhattan is a different story. Don't worry, though, because I'm here to help.

Seasonal variations

If you don't have a date set just yet, you should know that the rental market in NYC is seasonal. Consider timing your arrival. Try and avoid the rush in late summer when students saturate the market. After Thanksgiving through to spring is the best time to pick up a good deal.

Surviving when you first arrive

Unless you have a friend's couch to sleep on, your first few days will be expensive and frustrating as you try to find your own place. A hostel will cost you around $350 per week, while an AirBnB apartment will be about $600+. However, if you're on a budget, there is a far better option.

In Upper Manhattan, especially in Harlem, there are numerous brokers that offer cheap weekly room rentals (usually for Hispanic migrants). There's an advance on the broker's fee to the tune of $150, and you'll also have to stump one week's security (which you'll eventually get back), but the good news is the rooms are only about $150-$200 a week, payable weekly, and all you need is a valid ID. So, for less than $500, you're in the door and have your own bed. Compare this with a typical lease requiring you to jump through hoops, sign contracts, and provide three to four months upfront. This typically adds up to thousands of dollars...and you still have to buy a bed to sleep on!

Unfortunately, you get what you pay for. Most of these accommodations are very basic. Expect to share the apartment with a bunch of other renters and a live-in owner, who is almost always an old Dominican woman who can barely speak any English. You'll be given a room with a bed, access to a toilet, and usually a kitchen. I've also read horror stories online about these rentals: shady brokers, bed bugs, mice, living with drug dealers, etc.

All that said, you can get lucky. My brother, for example, was only paying \$135 a week for room with a double bed that was only half a block from the 1 train stop on Broadway and 137th Street. His landlady also had zero problems with smoking weed and late night guests! In fact, his situation was so good that he didn't even bother finding another place until eight months later. The moral of the story is to make sure you shop around, and make sure your broker shows you a few options before you make a decision.

A list of week-by-week brokers:

- Delta Room Rentals (verified): deltaroomrentals.com; 212-281-3202; 3644 Broadway, corner of 150th St.

- NYC Rooms for Rent: nycrooms4rent.com; 1800-964-3360; 606 West 145th St.

- Jah Rooms For Rent: 212-544-0099; 140 Amsterdam Avenue.

- Room Rental Zone: 646-351-6502; 601 West 182nd St.

Leasing

As I mentioned previously, securing a lease is an expensive and arduous process requiring several prerequisites. The average monthly rent in Manhattan is now a whopping \$4,000 a month. On top of providing a security deposit and your first and last month's rent, many apartments are sold through brokers, requiring *another* month's rent for a 'finder's fee.' The best way to avoid this is to search under "no-fee" apartments on Craigslist. However, your options will be limited. In certain neighbors, such as Astoria or Central Manhattan, you will find it almost impossible to find a place without going through a broker. That said, some brokers charge less than others, and some even waive their fees altogether depending on the deal. It depends on where you're looking and who you're dealing with.

Subletting: The Smart Choice

As an out-of-towner, it's a lot less hassle—and usually more affordable—to move in with somebody who already has a lease. There are tons of leasers looking for roommates online, and their only major requirement is that you're cool. Go to Craigslist and look under "Rooms/Shared" or visit the 'Gypsy Housing' page on Facebook. The latter is also great for short stays as well as sublets. The cheapest rooms you can find are usually around $700-900 a month. These are usually in the likes of Washington Heights or somewhere crappy in Brooklyn. If you're lucky, you can find something in this price range in Astoria, West Harlem, or the East Side. However, most rooms in the city average around $1,000-1,300 a month.

WHAT TO PACK

An unlocked smartphone

Obviously, this only applies to non-Americans. Most mobile phone companies offer short-term contracts with unlimited calls and data for as little as $3 a day. You'd be an idiot to skimp on this. Trust me, in New York, Google Maps will become your new best friend. Having a local number is also a must for arranging hookups and communicating with friends.

A fetching hat

Okay, it doesn't have to be a hat, but every NYC player worth his salt knows that to succeed is this city, it helps to separate yourself from the crowd. A dapper necktie, a pocket square, a striking shirt: *something!* Never underestimate the power of a little peacocking. Women respond to it here.

A portable speaker

Preferably, get a Bluetooth one so you can control it wirelessly through your phone—nothing looks cooler than when Marvin Gaye suddenly starts playing the moment you enter the room. My Bluetooth speaker is probably my favorite travel gadget and only cost me $20 on Amazon. Make sure you also have the right playlist and are prepared when the time comes.

Scented candles

It sounds cheesy, but they work wonders. Skin looks great under candlelight, and the resulting ambiance and scent of vanilla can turn a cockroach infested sty into a romantic love nest. Pro tip from Mystery: try and get the girl to light the candles. Her active participation in the seduction builds compliance.

Condoms and sexcessories

Massage oil, Astroglide, that seven-piece bondage kit you got online: throw 'em in the bag! Whatever your kinks are, you'll find that girls in New York are more than willing to indulge you. Hell, some of them even carry around their own toys. Make sure you bring condoms, too, and be sure to wrap it up. Too many girls in the city regularly have unprotected sex on one-night stands.

RECOMMENDED APPS

NYC Bus and Subway Maps

Pretty self-explanatory.

NYC Subway Times [MTA/BETA]

This app gives you real-time train arrival information so you'll know exactly when your train is coming. This way you'll know if you have time to grab a pizza slice at 4 a.m.

Lyft or Uber

The best way to catch a ride in the city. They'll pick you up at any location and you have all your driver's info. Lyft Line and Uber Pool services also offer shared rides with predetermined fares that are often cheaper than a taxi.

Dating Apps

Tinder, OkCupid, Jswipe (Jewish Tinder), Badoo, Hot or Not etc. With such a high population density, there are few better cities for hooking up online.

THE GIRLS

*"The city of sin is a pity on a whim.
Good girls gone bad, the city's filled with 'em."*

- Jay Z

OVERVIEW

New York is a sexual smorgasbord. Beautiful women from all over the world flock here to 'make it' and fulfill their *Sex in the City* fantasy. They come here with rose-tinted glasses, picturing themselves under the bright lights of Broadway, shopping for chic couture, and romantic strolls through Central Park with some dreamy guy who makes her vagina tingle.

However, in reality, they usually end up jaded, struggling to pay the rent, and binge drinking to the point that they're sniffing coke off some bartender's dick in a bathroom stall.

Ah, New York, New York. But in all seriousness, not all women who come here indulge in vice so readily. It would be folly of me not to make some distinctions. In truth, the vaginal tapestry of New York is so rich and varied that unraveling it would take a dozen lifetimes. Laquisha from the Bronx is nothing like Amy from Ohio or Ling from Beijing. But they all have vaginas, and we're men, which is why we're going to package these gals into neat little boxes to help you get laid! The politically correct brigade will no doubt scoff at the generalizations and caricatures that follow, insisting that these women are all unique little snowflakes, but here in New York, you'll never see greater examples of people conforming to certain stereotypes. That said, what does the "average" New York woman look like according to the stats?

The Average New York Woman

Meet Jen. She is the average New York woman. Jen is 35 years old, with light skin, dark hair, and brown eyes. She is 5'4'' in height and weighs 145lbs, considerably less than the average American woman, and she tends to dress better too. She's pretty average-looking, but most men would consider banging Jen after a few pints at last call.

Despite not having a bachelor's degree, Jen managed to land a career for a large corporation where she makes a respectable $47,600 a year: enough to comfortably pay the bills at her small apartment in Brooklyn. The rest of her income is spent on clothes, going out to bars and restaurants, and GrubHub.

Jen has never been married. She has had many suitors, but sadly, her favorites soon tire of her because she's an iPhone-addicted, selfie-taking, reality-show-bingeing bore who knows very little about the world outside her rat-race life spent slithering underground on the island of Manhattan. Out of the twenty or so men Jennifer recalls having slept with, the majority of these were in her twenties. Most of the time she did not use a condom. She hopes to one day find her Mr. Right, but despite her ticking biological clock, she's quite happy being single and playing the dating game. Nowadays, she usually waits until the third date to spread her legs, but still indulges in the occasional one night stand. She considers herself pretty kinky, having sent nudies via text and had public sex on at least one occasion.

Jen shares one thing in common with other women in her city: the New York Mindset.

The New York Mindset

Women in the city are highly sexualized. Living in a densely populated multicultural city such as New York, even the most conservative girls are not immune from liberalization. Unaccountable and less concerned with their reputation, they become less inhibited and freer to express themselves: for better or worse. As such, previous sexual taboos are paid less credence. Never in my life have I encountered so many women open to bisexuality, threesomes, public sex, BDSM, and other kinks.

Promiscuity is rampant and, in some cases, excessive. Some of these women ride the cock carousel so hard that before they know it they've YOLOed themselves in their mid-forties—or the nearest abortion clinic. I once slept with a woman who had a blackboard above her bed that was covered with the signatures of her former conquests (at her request, of course, as if her vagina was petitioning to become mayor of Whoretown). She also owned no less than seven dildos and her roommate, a bartender at a sex club, got off on puncturing her back with metal hooks and hanging her body from the ceiling by her stretched skin. Quite a team, eh?

Public sex is another penchant of New Yorkers. According to Time Out magazine, 63% of locals have reported getting busy in public. My experience matches this, having had countless romps with women in bar bathrooms, public parks, and behind dumpsters. I've even had a woman give me a blowjob on a bench on Amsterdam Avenue in full view of pedestrians.

Despite such sexual profligacy, this does not necessarily mean it's easy to get laid. Women here are choosy. New York breeds hordes of fearless thirsty men who'll approach anything with a heartbeat, inflating females egos to mesospheric levels and lowering the bar to the point where even mediocre, aging fatties are constantly propositioned. With literally millions of men around, the choice for women is overwhelming. Even if your game is tight and you're dating models or actresses, it's only a matter of time before some dude with more wealth, status, and better looks comes along to try his luck. This reality begets some undesirable female traits. Severe flakiness, harlotry, and duplicity are pervasive, and even if you do find a girl worth keeping around, she will love with one foot out the door, always wondering if she can do better.

To put it simply, aside from a few hopeless romantics, most women in New York just don't give a fuck.

THE STATS

Ladies of New York

City Population: 8.4 Million

53% Female
47% Male

Est. number of single women aged 20-35:

729,500

Race
2% Other
29% Hispanic
33% White
23% Black
13% Asian

RATIO OF
Single Men to
Single Women
Ages 20 - 34

0.67 - 0.75
0.76 - 0.95
0.96 - 1.05
1.06 - 1.25
1.26 - 1.81

Kingsbridge
Baychester
Co-op City
Mosholu
Pelham Gardens
Washington Heights
Fordham
Morrisania
Morningside Heights
Highbridge
Parkchester
Throgs Neck
Harlem
Mott Haven
Hunts Point
East Harlem
College Point
UWS
UES
Midtown
Astoria
Chelsea
Jackson Heights
Flushing
Bayside
Midtown East
LIC
Greenwich Village
Sunnyside
Elmhurst
Little Neck
Financial District
LES
Forest Hills
Hillcrest
Williamsburg
Middle Village
Bushwick
Downtown BK
Bed-Stuy
Kew Gardens
Jamaica
Red Hook
Park Slope
Crown Heights
East New York
Ozone Park
Sunset Park
Brownsville
Rosedale
East Flatbush
Borough Park
Bay Ridge
Flatbush
Canarsie
Bensonhurst
Flatlands
Sheepshead Bay
Rockaways
Coney Island

NYCEDC

Source: http://www.nycedc.com/blog-entry/singles-nyc

Ethnic Enclaves

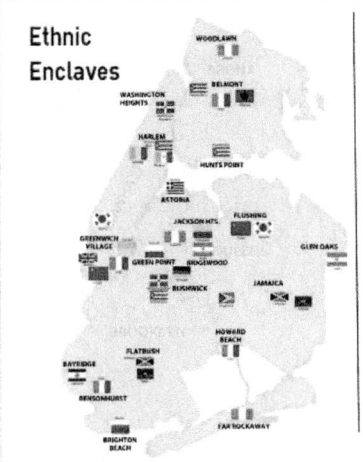

55.8 Million

The number of tourists in 2014

Where from?

1. United Kingdom	1,1 mil
2. Canada	1,1 mil
3. Brazil	895k
4. France	697k
5. China (PRC)	646k
6. Australia	619k
7. Germany	608k
8. Italy	464k
9. Spain	383k
10. Japan	337k

Foreign-born Population

1. Dominican Republic	380k
2. China*	350k
3. Mexico	186k
4. Jamaica	169k
5. Guyana	140k
6. Ecuador	138k
7. Haiti	94k
8. Trinidad and Tobago	88k
9. India	77k
10. Russia	76k
11. Bangladesh	75k
12. Korea	73k
13. Colombia	66k
14. Ukraine	60k
15. Poland	58k
16. Philippines	51k
17. Italy	49k
18. Pakistan	40k
19. United Kingdom	34k
20. El Salvador	33k

38%
of New Yorkers are foreign-born

Source: U.S census Bureau
*Taiwan and Hong Kong included.

THE NINE TYPES

"In New York, you have to go through 100 girls to find one that's worth a 2nd date," I once Tweeted. While beautiful women are plentiful, their characters are often lacking. Prepare to have your head wrecked by some of the most annoying women on the planet. Most of these women are only good for one thing, but there are a few diamonds in the rough. The following is a breakdown of common types you're likely to encounter in the city. Nearly every single girl you meet will be a variation or combination of the characters below.

The Careerist

One of the most common characters in the city, especially in Manhattan. The Careerist is your typical college graduate in her mid-twenties to early forties. With a few exceptions, the majority of these women hold a boring mid-level position as a corporate drone.

The Careerist is educated, independent, and has a strong sense of entitlement. Her primary focus in New York is work, not starting a family. She has a very level-headed, realistic approach to relationships. Having already experienced a plethora of penis, she has learned to be more cautious with men, having been pumped and dumped one too many times in the city. She still enjoys dating and casual sex, but doesn't get too involved unless she thinks a guy has serious potential. She prefers to wait until after the first date for sex, and tells men 'she's not like that,' showcasing token resistance before you handcuff her to the bedpost on your next meetup.

If she remains single, the Careerist morphs into a familiar form known as **The Cougar**. And as the wrinkles deepen and the laughter fades, the cougar becomes the **Cat Woman**, and then she dies, only remembered by her closest friend, Mittens.

Where to find her

You normally see this type of girl suited up during the day, mingling with colleagues at happy hour after work in Midtown, and washing back mimosas with her besties at brunch on weekends. Some nights you'll also find her in her local neighborhood bar, drowning away the mundane monotony of everyday life on the grind.

The College Student

Did you know that NYC has more college students than the population of Boston? NYU has over 50,000 students alone. Ivy leaguer Columbia has another 30,000, and CUNY (City University of New York) adds nearly another 500,000 students to the pot! That, my friends, is hell of a lot of fresh meat to feast upon. NYC is also the number one destination in the U.S. for international students, with Chinese, Indian, South Korean, Canadian, and Taiwanese students making up the largest representations. Young, unattached, and sexually curious, the college student is a staple in every local player's rotation.

The most common college girl is your average, middle-class American attending public university and surviving on either a student loan, financial aid, a part-time job or goodwill from her parents. While these girls are everywhere in the city, they're dispersed and largely invisible. Due to their tentative financial status, you don't often meet these girls out partying, unless there's $1 beers or it's student night somewhere.

Next, we have the rich Ivy League nerds of Columbia. Having lived in the neighborhood and dated a few of these bookworms, I can say with authority that these are the most boring group. This is best exemplified by nightlife in the area, which is so poor and underwhelming you'd never think there was a university nearby. This makes hunting Columbians a little frustrating, but on the upside there's a lot of ethnic diversity: 36% White, 29% Asian/Asian American, 13% Latino, 12% Black, and 7% other. Also among these are several thousand international students.

Finally, moving on from the nerds, the other significant group is the equally pretentious, but slightly "cooler" gals of NYU, who can out-party their college rivals any day of the week. Like Columbia, NYU also boasts a diverse campus with a huge number of international students. However, dispel your illusions; it mainly caters to spoilt white hipsters whose parents have too much money. (Especially privileged are those attending the Tisch School of the Arts, getting daddy to shell out $60,000 a year for their little angel to "express herself.") But entitled attitudes aside, NYU has a very favorable ratio of females to males (almost 60/40), and it's widely known that out of those men, a large percentage identity as homosexual. In short, NYU's female body suffers from dick-drought, making them prime targets for a good rogering.

Where to find her
The area around NYU and Washington Park is the epicenter of student nightlife, and both Greenwich and East Village are dotted with college hangouts. Well-known strips include Bleecker Street and MacDougal Street. The other main student area is east of the 2nd Avenue stop on the Lower East Side, mainly the bars around Houston Street and Stanton Street.

The Small-Town Dreamer

She's a small town girl in her twenties who came to the big city to "make it" and maybe, just maybe, find that "special guy" in the process. She's a romantic who wants the New York fairy-tale. She didn't come for some office job or to study: she has bigger plans! When asked, she defines herself as either an aspiring actress, model, musician, or writer. However, in reality, she usually ends up paying her bills by working in the service industry.

She is open-minded, a little naive, and still exploring her sexuality. Alas, her new life in New York is not quite as she imagined back home in middle America or Bishkek, Uzbekistan. She's become a little jaded, misses her friends and family, and had her heart stomped on once or twice while sowing her wild oats. All that said, she's still eager to meet new people and experience all the city has to offer. This makes her more approachable than other New Yorkers and fun for casual dating, but tread lightly. Ultimately alone in the city, and working a temporary job, this type has a tendency to become emotionally dependent. Some of these girls do genuinely go on to "make it" and do big things, but the majority of them are drifters who will eventually give up and move on.

Where to find her

More than half the city's population is born outside New York, so these girls are everywhere. She's the girl serving cocktails, reading in the park, or staring out the coffee shop window. These girls tend to be Manhattan-centric, but due to budgetary constraints, many find themselves living in hoods in Brooklyn, Queens, or Uptown.

The Latina Flame

Nearly a third of New Yorkers are Hispanic or what they call "Spanish." Dominicans and Puerto Ricans dominate the community, who combined number nearly 1.5 million. The next biggest groups are Mexicans, Ecuadorians, Colombians, and Salvadorians.

Leaving out the more indigenous looking types, without a doubt, the typical New York Latina harbors more sex appeal than any others you'll meet in the city. If you're an ass man like myself, some of them have bodies that will make your jaw drop. When I visited the Dominican Republic, I wasn't impressed with the quality, but now I know why—all the good-looking ones emigrated to New York! Furthermore, these bootylicious babes are all over the city and ripe for the picking. But while they're more sensual and feminine than their black and white sisters (provided they're not ratchet types), these spicy specimens come with a warning. Jealous and often dramatic, many of them are bat-shit crazy. Date them for fiery sex, but manage expectations early. Latin New Yorkers tend to be a little bit more traditional than others and are less tolerant of sharing their men.

Where to find her

As I mentioned, one in three people in New York are Hispanic, so you see these girls everywhere you turn. At night, you can find the best of them concentrated on Dyckman Street in Washington Heights. Other hot spots include Jackson Heights, Corona, and Spanish Harlem. Most Mexican restaurants also convert into disco bars on weekends, too.

The Privileged Princess

The type of character that inspired *Gossip Girl* and *Clueless*. She's a privileged, narcissistic daddy's girl who lives in a nice neighborhood, usually on the Upper East or West side. She's typically young, white, well-dressed, and can be found buried in her smartphone, making hashtags for her gluten-free salad pics. However, she is most recognizable by her whiny, nagging speech riddled with vocal fry and upward inflection which is, you know, like... Totes. Super. Annoying.

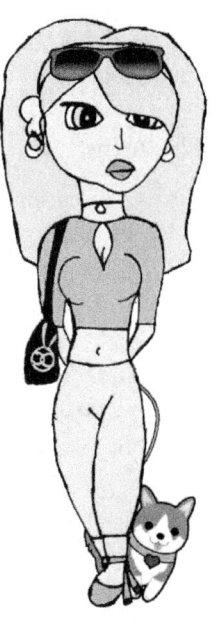

The Privileged Princess is commonly found in the form of a WASP (White Anglo-Saxon Protestant) or her stingier, bigoted sister-in-aristocracy, the JAP (Jewish American Princess). The city hosts the largest Jewish community outside of Israel.

Your typical WASP is an air-headed, fun-loving social butterfly who likes to party. She can be a bit of fun in the sack, but she's usually uber-flaky, completely self-centered, and prone to chlamydia. The JAP is a little more old-school. She dresses more conservatively, at least pretends not to sleep around as much, keeps herself in shape, and is less likely to have Insomnia Cookies on speed dial. Some JAPs are a bit narrow-minded when it comes to dating non-Jewish guys, but like all privileged princesses, you can pick them up if you have style, charisma, and know where to find them.

Where to find her

During the day, you'll see her heading to yoga class or shopping at Whole Foods. At night, you'll find her at high-end clubs or a trendy restaurant with girlfriends, either mindlessly gossiping or on Yelp complaining that her lime juice wasn't freshly squeezed. If you want the JAP variety, just look for the group huddling over a single cocktail while drinking water.

The Asian

Nearly one in eight people in NYC are of Asian descent. The vast majority you'll meet in the city will be either Chinese or Korean. Numbering well over 700,000, New York City has the largest population of Chinese outside of Asia. Add to that another 100,000 Koreans and you have an Asiaphile's oasis. There is also a sizable number of South Asians from India, Pakistan, and Bangladesh. Most of these girls are foreign-born or first generation and unlike many other New Yorkers, they tend to be more culturally insular and immune from Western indoctrination. While all of these cultures are no doubt extremely diverse, their women have very similar traits, provided the girl is not a "Banana": an Americanized Asian who is yellow on the outside but white on the inside and can't even speak her mother tongue.

Unlike her relatively boorish American counterpart, this girl maintains a feminine, demure disposition. A more respectful approach is required. She is more reserved than others, so don't automatically expect a one-night stand. These girls also tend to go out in large, mixed groups, so she may be mindful of being judged by her peers. Isolating before escalating is crucial, and even kissing in public is something that she might be reluctant to do. This can throw some guys off, but the key here is to be persistent.

Where to find her

Chinatown and Koreatown, obviously. Any bar in Flushing, Queens. Bubble tea shops and karaoke joints. Third Floor Cafe on 5th Avenue or Circle Club nears Times Square. For Indians, the Park Nightclub in Chelsea. For Tibetans and Nepalese, check out Sean Og's in Woodside.

The Ratchet Chick

"Ratchet" is a term you'll hear a lot in New York. It's often used as a euphemism for anything considered ghetto, but when applied to females, it usually refers to an African-American or Hispanic woman from a lower-class background who looks and acts like a diva, despite being uneducated, talent-less, and unable to construct grammatically correct sentences. Often jobless and rarely graduating from 'side-bitch' status in her relationships, her primary sense of self-worth is determined by the amount of 'likes' she receives from snapping her booty on Instagram. It's sad, but true.

You'll see her in clubs and lounges, usually with a loud-mouthed cohort hollering in Ebonics and dropping the N-word incessantly, displaying about as much class as that of an Afghan schoolgirl under Taliban rule. She may not be very sophisticated, but her excessive confidence, thick buttocks, ostentatious dress and trashy tattoos all hold a certain, stripper-esque sex appeal that still makes you want to nail her ghetto ass.

Some of these girls are reluctant to date outside their race, often judged for doing so by their peers, but the New York variety are more open-minded, provided you approach them alone or in small all-female groups. Just remember to wrap up because you want *no* part in this girl's future, for hers is a life destined for welfare checks, multiple baby daddies, and ungovernable weight gain; grab her while she's young and firm.

Where to find her

Certain venues cater to these types, but you can find them in any place playing hip-hop. She'll likely be taking selfies with her friends, ordering Patron Margaritas—without tipping, of course— and twerking that bubble butt to the latest Nicki Minaj track.

The Hipster

The Hipster is usually a young, middle-class light-skinned girl who lives in neighborhoods like Williamsburg, Bushwick, West Harlem, or other any other place yet to experience gentrification (meaning the rents are cheap). She's usually easy to spot. Normally, these girls don't conform to what they would call "conventional ideals of beauty," meaning they're kinda ugly, basically. To compensate, the Hipster tries to "peacock" and be different. She achieves this by getting a bunch of crappy personalized tattoos, facial piercings, and purposely dressing in an unflattering, un-sexy manner, usually involving vintage clothes or wearing "quirky" accessories like thick-framed  eyeglasses and pieces from her grandmother's wardrobe. Bonus points for androgynous clown hair. As a general rule, the more liberal she is, the uglier she'll be, too. (You'll almost never meet one that's above a 7.)

Williamsburg is the hipster capital of the world, so you'll undoubtedly run into some of this ilk while bar-crawling. She an artsy, liberal know-it-all who strives for non-conformity, despite owning the latest iPhone and parroting the exact same moralistic opinions as other social justice warriors she meets, on everything from veganism to push bikes. She talks about "double standards," "privilege," "street harassment," and lectures people every time they use words like "slut" or "whore." She's the useful idiot who, to quote Roosh V, "believes in an extreme left-wing ideology that combines feminism, progressivism, and political correctness." Of course, the Hipster would also disagree with that statement because she doesn't believe in labels. "You can't stereotype people and put them into boxes!" she'll protest. This attitude can get annoying, but bear with it. Due to her 'progressive' views of sexuality, she's low-hanging fruit. So smile and nod, gentlemen. Smile and nod. If you must speak, tell her about that band she's never heard of, or your time in Southeast Asia teaching orphans how to hand-paint. Dazzle her with your knowledge of obscure Ethiopian honey wines and your views on the gentrification of Puerto Rican fishing villages. Then nail and bail, bro, because this bitch make your ears bleed.

Where to find her

College campuses. Whole Foods or any organic vegetable store. Starbucks, because even though she's anti-globalization, she just loooooves her chai lattes. You'll find her everywhere except a nightclub where she has to compete with members of her sex who act like actual women. Instead, try any bar selling cheap PBRs.

The Trampy Tourist

With over 50 million visitors a year, New York City has the biggest turnover of pussy in the Western Hemisphere. Aside from a brief period from January to mid-March, it's high season is all year round. Most of these female visitors come from elsewhere in North America, but millions also flock from overseas. The majority of these come from western Europe, but you'll also meet plenty of girls from Brazil, Australia, and East Asia.

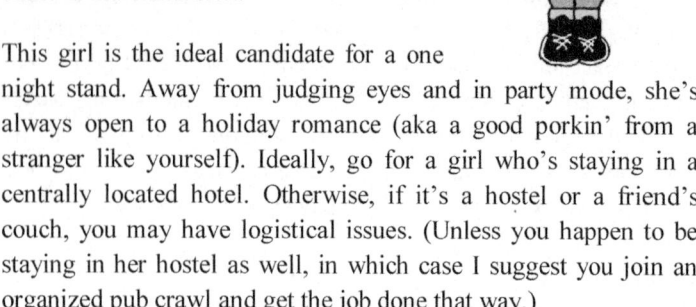

Unlike your average bore who just comes to the city to take Facebook profilers and is in bed early for the museums, the trampy tourist is a young bachelorette who is as interested in bar-hopping as she is sightseeing. Usually accompanied by her like-minded bff, she intends to make the most of her short visit. She's out to get shit-faced, dance until her feet hurt, and bathe in male attention.

This girl is the ideal candidate for a one night stand. Away from judging eyes and in party mode, she's always open to a holiday romance (aka a good porkin' from a stranger like yourself). Ideally, go for a girl who's staying in a centrally located hotel. Otherwise, if it's a hostel or a friend's couch, you may have logistical issues. (Unless you happen to be staying in her hostel as well, in which case I suggest you join an organized pub crawl and get the job done that way.)

The best way to bag the trampy tourist to be bold and direct. Unlike other girls in the city, she's not sticking around, so it's do or die.

Where to find her

The most obvious way to meet tourists is to use day game around the main tourist spots: Times Square, the High Line, Central Park, the 9/11 Memorial, Brooklyn Bridge, etc. At night, try any popular venue in central Midtown, Greenwich, or East Village.

GAME

"Since there's 8 million people in the city, if you're not getting laid, you're a fucking asshole."

- Joe, a 20-something homeless guy

Adapting to the New York City dating scene can be tricky. In this concrete jungle, competition is fierce, and females are very selective. Picking up here can be a little frustrating at first, but once you crack the code, you'll be rotating so much pussy you'll wish your local STD clinic offered memberships. To learn how to win the game here, we must first analyze the playing field.

THE COMPETITION

The first step is understanding your opponents. Compared to most cities, men in New York are more assertive and aggressive when it comes to picking up women. I can think of few cities where men exhibit such little approach anxiety. Leave a cute girl alone in a crowded bar to go the bathroom and you're almost guaranteed she'll have some guy hovering over her by the time you get back. Even if you've been making out, some guys will see this and *still* hit on your date.

Guys here are not only brave but extremely persistent, pursuing the same girl even after getting rejected multiple times. They believe that a soft "no" can be turned into a "yes" with a little coaxing—or another shot of Jameson—and they're not wrong for thinking that way. A little token resistance is required for ladies to survive in New York, and such flip-flopping happens all the time. Nonetheless, too many guys here can't seem to recognize a genuine rejection unless they literally get told to go fuck themselves.

While this kind of thirsty behavior inflates female egos and creates a very competitive environment, the good news is that most guys in New York have shitty game and are clueless when it comes to attraction. They give too many compliments, have poor conversations skills, and talk about money too much. Their best method of seduction is buying a girl drinks, getting them wasted, and luring them home with drugs. Most of these dudes hold down banal jobs and have limited experience beyond their worker bee life of the big city. The exceptions (those with brains and interesting lives and professions) are usually intellectual hipster types who exude about as much masculinity as a pack of tampons. In contrast, those with muscles and swag are usually lower-class hood types who dress poorly, come off too strong, and ultimately get looked down on by the finicky females here.

To conclude, the lack of decent competition combined with the favorable sex ratio leaves the average guy with basic game at an easy advantage in New York City.

ONLINE GAME

With millions of people concentrated in such a small space, there are few places more suited to online dating than New York City. You can find exactly what you want here. Looking for a bisexual, mixed race 19-year-old who lives within a 5-mile radius?—You got it! I'm a night hunter by nature, but I can't deny I've had some impressive results by using dating sites and apps. Some of the sexiest (and kinkiest) girls I've hooked up with here I've met online. However, overall, the standard of girls you'll end up meeting online won't be a patch on the talent you can pull at night.

Furthermore, many of these internet chicks also end up being mentally or emotionally unstable—great in the bed, but mad in the head. Other potential hazards of hunting online include catfish, secret fatties, and ladyboys. Be wary.

If you're only visiting NYC for a short time, using online game is probably your most reliable method for getting laid. You can do this by using location dependent swipe apps when you arrive, but a superior method is *pipelining:* arranging dates online *before* you arrive. Regardless of how you choose to go about it, there are tons of options to choose from: Tinder, OkCupid, Skout, Plenty of Fish, Match, Hot-or-not, Badoo, J-swipe, Coffee-meets-bagel, Grouper, Lulu—the list goes on.

Swipe Apps

First, let's talk about swipe apps such as Tinder. These apps allow users to browse nearby females and reject or approve them based on a single picture by swiping left or right. While this no-bullshit approach helps you filter out the ugly ducklings at lighting speed, these apps have the lowest success rates. Any idiot with a smartphone can set up an account in 30 seconds with minimum investment, and because of this, most women use the app to feed their ego rather than for actual dating, making the swipe-to-bang ratio pretty poor.

Some of these apps are better than others. For my research, I used several popular apps in various neighborhoods. I used a profile picture that was rated 7 out of 10 on the website hotornot.com. After indiscriminately swiping right for hundreds of women, I measured my match rates in a 48-hour period. I found that despite its popularity, Tinder actually yielded some of the *lowest* match and response rates compared to other apps. Just 0.7%. Compare this to the response rates from J-swipe (Jewish Tinder) and Hot-or-Not which yielded 6% and 8%, respectively. Furthermore, the advantage that Tinder enjoyed because of its sheer numbers has been marginalized since the company's recent introduction of a paywall that restricts the amount of "likes" one can give unless they fork over cash.

Hacking Location-Based Apps

One big flaw of swipe apps is that they are usually location dependent and only allow you to search for women in your local vicinity. They don't allow you to 'pipeline' before you arrive, meaning you waste time when you first touchdown. Tinder Plus has recently introduced 'Passport Mode' to solve this problem, however, you can do this for free using the following hack. Download an app called 'Tinder from everywhere.' This allows you create mock locations on your phone and essentially fool Tinder and any other dating apps that rely on your location.

Dating Sites

Leaving aside swipe apps, my top pick for online game is OKCupid. It's a little corny, perhaps, but it's a lot better than Plenty of Fish. I've had my best results from there both in terms of quantity and quality. There are a lot more fuglies to sift through than other apps/sites, but it's way more legit. Most of the women on the site have put some effort into creating a profile and are more serious about meeting people in real life. Also, not only can you filter by proximity, but by things like race, sexuality, and height too. You can even search for girls who smoke weed and speak Swahili if you want!

The only downside I've found with OKCupid is that the women are more likely to be emotionally unstable or have mental issues— unlike the more 'normal' girls you'll meet on Tinder. You've been warned.

While I endorse OKCupid, I should also mention that older players have reported having more success on Match.com.

DAY GAME

I'm not going to try and bullshit you, I'm not a big day game guy—but don't worry, I've got you guys covered. As part of my research, I reached out to the experts.

I spoke with Steve, founder of nycdaygame.com, a professional dating coach who specializes in day game. The following contains edited excerpts from an extensive interview.

Steve, tell us about yourself. How long have you been doing day game?

I've switched to day gaming a few years back, and I've been coaching men on how to confidently meet and attract women in New York City for over a year now. It's been going great, and I love what I do.

What are the three biggest mistakes you see guys making?

The number one mistake is NOT approaching in the first place—or hesitating. A lot of guys tend to think too much and get in their own head. I teach guys to make the approach an automatic response, so they leave no time or mental debate.

The next mistake I see is when guys *do* approach, they don't present themselves in a confident way. They're so nervous that they're stuttering or saying silly stuff. The only solution is just to push them to keep doing it and doing it until they become comfortable and smoother with it.

The third mistake is when a guy manages to talk to a girl for a little bit and they either eject themselves or just let the conversation die down. They don't close or get a phone number, failing to follow through and turn it into something. A girl can like the guy, but if he is scared to ask the question, he leaves with nothing. You have to ask every time and assume she likes you.

What's better: direct or indirect?

I'm a big fan of the direct approach. Some guys are more comfortable with it, but I've tested everything, and I've found direct works better. Indirect will get you into more conversations, but it's less likely those conversations will become sexual. It creates a barrier because at some point you have to transition from a normal conversation into: 'Hey I like you. Let's hang out.' With direct you're clear for the get-go. You're being honest, and girls don't have a chance to classify you as a potential friend or non-sexual. Furthermore, if the girl is just walking down the street, it seems unnatural to just catch up with and stop her just to ask an indirect question. It makes you appear socially maladjusted.

How do you get the conversation rolling? Give us some tips.

As I said, I'm a fan of being direct. Having done, taught, and seen so many approaches, I've noticed certain patterns work better. The best I've found is to let a girl walk past me, then catch up with her and get her to stop by saying, "Hey, excuse me." The biggest thing is to *make sure they stop*. If you don't stop and just start walking with them and try to talk to her, you've established they're taking the lead, and you're in a submissive follower role trying to get her attention. It's a bad dynamic, and you usually look like a creep.

Once you get her to stop, the next biggest thing is your non-verbal communication. Your eye contact, tonality, and body language all have to be solid. It's okay to be a *little* bit nervous—that shows authenticity—but you should still project confidence.

In terms of actual conversation, I usually talk about what just happened. I say, "I noticed you walking past me, and you caught my eye. I thought you looked pretty cute, so I wanted to come over here and meet you and see if you're cool." At this point, I've already given them a small compliment, and I'm getting them to qualify themselves. And really, this is healthy. After you do this a lot, you realize you don't want to take out every cute girl you meet. You want to qualify them and make sure you connect, and your personalities match a little bit. Then I take it from there. So basically, to get into a conversation in three steps: Stop, compliment, and then ask her about her personality. But all that said, 80% of it is your non-verbal communication.

[Note Steve makes a *statement* when referring to her personality. He does not ask her a question, yet still manages to get her talking.]

What's the best way to escalate during the day?

It's different for each guy. A lot of guys try to get sex as fast possible by talking to the girl for a longer length of time, then inviting them for an instant date—for coffee or ice cream—and then try to get them back to their place. It's definitely possible and I know a ton of guys who do it, but in New York people have places to be and an instant date isn't always viable. My theory is it's better to go for a two-date plan. I approach. I talk to them for a few minutes. I make it fun, make it flirtatious, and make very clear my sexual or romantic interest. And then I get their number and follow up with a low-key date later on. The second date I invite them over to my place to "watch a movie" and establish a sexual relationship.

Do you alter you approach depending on the girl? What if she's a tourist? Or a different race?

Some of the questions I like to ask is "What are you up to today?" or "What are you doing here?" That tends to yield a lot of useful information. If she says she's only here for a few days, I know she's not worth my time unless I can go for a quick hook-up. Otherwise, I don't alter my approach. Every girl responses to confidence.

Where are the best daytime locations to pick up in NYC?

I find the best places to pick up *quality* women are lower volume places like bookstores, the supermarket, or on the subway. That's more for guys who live here. If you're looking for volume, the stereotypical spot is Union Square, but that can be over-saturated with other day gamers. I like the parks: Madison Square Park, Central Park, Bryant Park, and especially Washington Square Park by NYU. Near any college campus on a weekday is also phenomenal. The Fashion Institute on 27th is great. Grand Central and Penn Station are also good places for lots of people.

[For tourists, check out the 9/11 memorial or Brooklyn Bridge.]

Do you think day game in NYC differs from other cities?

There's probably a few differences. In New York, the pace is very go-go-go. People are very focused on their careers. In the U.K, for example, the guys doing day game are more polite and soft-spoken. In New York, you got to be a little more loud, more to the point, and get to it quicker. In the end, though, people are people. They're either going to like you or not. There's probably a lot more similarities than differences.

***

So there you have. Aside from all of these obvious places that Steve and I mentioned in this section, the *best* places are always the ones nearest your accommodation. Major points of interest with always have more prospects, but targeting a few cuties hanging out in your local bagel joint or coffee shop is always more valuable to you.

NIGHT GAME

Night game is my area of expertise and where I've had the vast majority of my success in NYC—sometimes dragging back several girls a week to my place. The following is a breakdown of the most important things you need to know for a successful nocturnal hunt.

Location, location, location

When it comes to night game, by far the most important thing to know is this: getting laid in New York is like getting take out—it's all about speed and convenience. Nothing will cock-block you harder than bad logistics. Girls in New York are lazy and apathetic. They won't travel ten blocks for pizza when there's a deli on the corner. They don't care how awesome you are; for them, it's all about what requires the least amount of effort. Try invite a Jersey girl back to Astoria or a Bushwick broad back to the Bronx and they'll laugh in your face. As for Manhattanites, you have a better chance getting your granny to twerk for YouTube than getting those girls to cross a river. The primal ape within her sees a large body of water and instinctively cowers back to the safety of the island interior. As such, the minute you mention you live in another borough, her vagina will dry up like the Sahara. Oh sure, you might get lucky once and awhile; she could be super desperate or have her own place nearby and invite *you* home—but you can't count on that.

The biggest piece of advice I can give anybody coming to NYC is *hunt locally*. That means that if you live in Brooklyn, party in Brooklyn. If you live Queens, party in Queens. And if you live in the Bronx, well, then you should consider moving.

Ideally, you want to be within a walk-able distance to your place or no longer than a ten-minute taxi ride away. Any farther than that and her interest level will plummet unless she happens to live in the same area and would be going back there anyway.

All of this means that you may have to shell out a little bit more for better accommodation. And if you don't like the sound of that you can go fuck yourself—literally—because that $200 a month you'll save living in West Bubbafuck, Brooklyn will ensure you get about as much pussy as a middle-aged Bangladeshi bathroom attendant.

Dealing with smaller venues

Most drinking spots in New York City are relatively small compared to other cities. This can cause issues. In larger venues with higher volume, approaching every cute woman you see is not usually a problem. You're invisible. However, in your typical pokey New York bar, this 'numbers game' strategy is hard to implement without setting off the creep alarm of every woman in the room. In such circumstances, instead of hunting around like a wild dog, I find it better to lay a trap and let the girls come to you. I do this by setting myself up in the 'Kill Zone'. This is the area of the bar where you're most likely to maximize your interactions with women while in a stationary position. Your best option is to sit on the bar stools nearest the ladies restroom. Here is where you usually get the most female traffic. If a girl needs to powder her nose or get a drink, there's a high probability she'll enter a striking distance. Like the spider, you patiently wait by your web, and sure enough, it's only a matter of time before a tasty treat flies by and gets stuck in your threads of trickery. Then it's simply a matter of crawling on top of your prey with your hairy legs and penetrating it's trembling body.

(You can find my video tutorial on the Kill Zone here: youtu.be/7WPJ8xTOQpc.)

The Golden Period

New Yorkers tend to do their drinking early. During the week, peak times in most bars are happy hour between 5 and 7 p.m., followed by the "late-night crowd" after nine—most of whom are at home in bed by 2 a.m. By one in the morning, most bars are dead or become total sausage-fests. You can find the odd straggler to take home at last call (I've done it many times), but there's a bit of luck involved unless you go to very specific places on certain nights. In my nightlife guide to follow, I provide a day-by-day breakdown on where you need to be.

Fridays, the momentum from happy hour crosses over into the night, so the earlier, the better. The golden period is 11 p.m. to 1 a.m. Saturday the party starts a lot later, but you should still to go out relatively early. You want to catch the single women while they're warming up in the bars, not at 3 a.m. in the club when they've already hooked up with somebody or had 20 guys already try their luck. On both weekend nights, also note the doors of better venues become increasingly difficult the later it gets.

On any given night, I recommend getting to your first bar by 10.30 p.m. at the latest.

Style of Game

Now that we've talked about the where and the when, let's talk about the *how*. A lot of you have probably read pick-up books like *The Game, The Venusian Arts Handbook,* or *Bang,* (and if you haven't, you should), so I'm not going to rehash the basics tenets of good game. I will, however, give advice on gaming in New York City, specifically.

The type of night game you should employ in New York is what I call **Racecar Game**.

Most guys in New York are terrible drivers. They come on too strong and are too direct. When they come on the track, they blast off at full throttle, lose control at the first corner, and crash and burn.

Other guys have the opposite problem. They move at a slower pace and navigate the course with ease, but in the end they don't shift up gears fast enough when they're on the straight to the finish line.

You need to hang back a little at the start. Let the speed freaks in front make their mistakes, but at the same time get ahead of the pack before they jostle for position on the last lap. Approach without hesitation, but don't sexualize the conversation too early. Keep it fun and neutral. Wait until you feel the bite before you move forward.

Forget about getting numbers; it's do or die in this city. Girls here dole out their number to any guy who asks for it out of politeness to avoid an awkward interaction. By the time you text her, you'll likely be reduced to another annoying vibrate alert, a blurry face in the cloud of cocks pining for her attention. At that stage, you've been regulated to the amateur circuit; there are so many people in the race that you're not even a contender. Even if you get some digits after making out with a girl, there's a high probability you'll never hear from her again. Don't take it personally. Understand that New York females have so many options that they just don't want to waste their time. As such, **the guys who clean up in New York are the ones who steer well, but speed even better**. It's the same night or take a hike. I don't care if you have to fuck her in a doorway or down an alleyway, just get 'er done. When you see the opportunity to make your move, you put that peddle to the mother-fuckin' floor. I understand that sometimes it's not always possible to seal the deal, but it's your job to get as far as you can, as fast as you can. If you can't pump her full of fluid during a bathroom pit stop, then do everything you can to get her back to your place that same night, because if you don't, there's a good chance you'll run out of gas and never cross the finish line.

Getting them back to your place

Preparation is key. Stock up on booze. Most 24-hour delis will sell you a six-pack at any time, so you're sorted if she's a beer drinker, but be prepared if she's not. Most wine and liquor stores close at ten p.m., so you might want to think about that beforehand. (Besides, with the price of booze in NYC, having a bottle of vodka at home comes in handy for pregaming.)

The next thing you should consider is drugs. This is obviously optional. In my experience, it seems like almost every girl in the city smokes weed, and a disheartening amount do cocaine, too. I'm not into coke, but I've seen first-hand the power it has on women. The line, "Wanna come back to my place and do blow?" has an alarming success rate among women of a certain breed. (A guy I lived with got almost *all* of his bangs from luring women back to snort lines of the living room table.) If coke is your thing, I'm not going to hate. However, personally, I find that inviting a girl back to smoke a joint works just as well and has a broader appeal. I don't even like smoking when I'm with a chick (it kills my libido), but I can't deny that it works wonders as bait. I just take a toke or two and let them do the smoking. Then it's party time.

Before you leave your place to go out, also try and make sure your room is clean and the lighting is low—or at least have candles at the ready (preferably scented). Have a speaker or a laptop set to play music the moment you walk into the room.

COOL DATE IDEAS

So maybe you've arranged a meet-up online, or maybe you're seeing a girl and it's her birthday, or maybe you just want to do something cool in the city and you wouldn't mind if someone tagged along. Here's a list of cool date ideas. Just keep in mind the basics: no dinner dates prior to sex, try and stick to drinks, and the closer you are to your place, the better.

Cheap & Sober

- A walk on the High Line or through Central Park.

- Free Tours by Foot offer several free walking tours and some pretty cheap food tours in various neighborhoods. *freetoursbyfoot.com*

- Any coffee shop off the beaten track that's not too crowded.

- Free kayaking on the Hudson. Check out *downtownboathouse.org*.

- A visit to a museum. I recommend the Natural History Museum. Entry is donation based.

- A trip to Coney Island (summer only). The rides cost a bit, but there's also a beach and plenty of other things to do along the boardwalk. Long Beach and Rockaway Beach are better alternatives if you're looking to soak up the sun, however.

- Watch a free movie in one of the city parks. They usually start at 8 p.m., but arrive early to get a spot. Google "Free Summer Movies NYC" for more info.

- B.Y.O.B. If you don't want to blow cash on boozing, they're several eateries and cigar bars that allow patrons to bring their own alcohol. Many wine spots also offer free corkage on quiet nights.

- Go rock climbing. There are a few options; I like the gym in Hell's Kitchen. Check out *mphc.com* for more info.

- Check out Groupon or Amazon local for deals on everything from archery to bike riding to wine tasting.

Cool Drink Dates

- Try some inventive, bespoke cocktails at one of the city's many hidden speakeasies. (See nightlife section.)

- Laugh your ass off at my favorite hangout *The Comedy Cellar* on MacDougal Street in Greenwich Village.

- Catch the view at one of the city's many rooftop bars. For dates, I recommend *230 Fifth* in Midtown East.

- Challenge her to some old-school video games at *Barcade,* ping pong at *Fat Cat,* or shuffleboard at the likes of *The Whiskey* or *At The Wallace* (boards games are also found in many bars).

- Go for drunk bowling at one of the cities bar and bowl hybrids around the city. Some of these places are a little overpriced, so check out happy hours and deals online. I like *Lucky Strike* on 12th Ave. There's also *The Gutter* and *Brooklyn Bowl* in Williamsburg.

A Special Occasion

- Shoot rifles at *The Westside Rifle and Pistol Range.*

- Take a helicopter tour.

- See a show. My top picks go to *The Book of Mormon* and *The Blue Man Group.*

- Jetski around Manhattan.

- Go sailing.

Travel the world without leaving the Island

Every neighborhood is well-stocked with Latin American, Thai, and European restaurants, but at these places you always feel like you're still in New York. Here are a few places I feel will give you an authentic out-of-the-country experience.

- Visit **Ethiopia**. I've been to almost every Ethiopian restaurant in the city and have liked them all. For an introduction, I recommended the *Tibs & Kitfo* special combo at *Awash* on the Upper West Side. They also have a place in East Village (but that one doesn't offer the combo).

- Visit **Afghanistan**. Smoke Shisha at atmospheric *Khyber Pass* on St. Marks.

- Visit **China**. Take a stroll through Chinatown, grab a cheap bite or some bubble tea, and feel like you're in the middle of Beijing. It really is a different world.

- Visit **Georgia**. Try some *khinkali* or sample Georgian wine at *Old Tbilisi Garden* or *Oda House*.

- Visit **Russia**. Choose from a myriad of unusually flavored vodka and raw meats at *Pravda, Russian Samovar* or *Russia Vodka Room*. There's also a Russian Banya (bathhouse) on the Lower East Side.

- Visit **Japan**. Cook your own meat at *Japanese BBQ,* get some noodles at one of the cool underground spots on St. Mark's Street, or grab some sushi at my favorite spot *Ageha* on 9th Ave. Sun-Thursday it's only $2 for beers and sake, so you can get-a serious-wee dwunk.

NIGHTLIFE

"There's something in the New York air that makes sleep useless."

- Some Dead Feminist

OVERVIEW

The city that never sleeps? I wish. It's a bit of a misnomer if you ask me. If anything, New York City needs to down a few Red Bulls.

In its heyday in the mid 90's, NYC may have earned that nickname, but things were a lot more lax back then. That was before Rudy Giuliani began to enforce 1920's cabaret laws, prohibiting more than three people from syncing up body movements to music at any one time unless the venue has a dance license (which is subject to permits and review by a pompous community boards). Sadly, the results of this are all too visible. Most nightclubs in New York don't have a designated dance floor, and many even have "no dancing allowed" signs. These archaic laws—along with skyrocketing rents—have choked the New York dance scene, and in its place, bottle service and gastropubs have taken over.

I could look past such worrying developments—or the fact that I can't party till sunrise like in the Med or drink in the street like in New Orleans or Berlin—but where NYC really loses brownie points is the midweek scene. On weekends New York is charged like a matador on methamphetamines, but from Sunday to Wednesday, most of the city is in a fucking coma. Pathetically, even my small home city of Dublin could rival NYC early in the week. Ultimately, this lull in the nightlife makes it seem a little underwhelming.

All that said, I still have to give it up for New York. Venue options are practically limitless, and the ability to grab a pint at 4 a.m. still puts the city well ahead of everywhere else in the U.S. and most foreign capitals. And luckily for you, your pal Mark Zolo has the scoop on where to go, even on the quiet nights! I've run the whole gambit of NYC nightlife, from bottle service with models at high-end rooftop clubs to downing $2 beer cans at dive bars with doorless toilets, and I'm here to steer you in the right direction.

TYPES OF VENUES

Choosing where to go out in New York City is daunting to the first-time visitor. There are so many different areas with so many options, each hosting different parties on different nights, and trends change fast. Even while writing this guide, with each draft I've had to add and delete venues because so many have come and gone.

On weekdays, only certain venues are worth checking out, but if you're going out on the weekend, you can find a party just about everywhere. Even your nearest hole-in-the-wall Mexican restaurant turns into a mini-disco on Friday and Saturday after midnight, with loud music and people dancing till the early morning.

Here's a list of typical venues you'll find in the city.

Dive Bars and College Spots

Dive bars are abundant in New York City. If you like cheap beer, an unpretentious vibe, and broke chicks, your best bet is Williamsburg and the Lower East Side (LES), followed by East Village. For those feeling a little more adventurous, another option is a pub crawl around the Jefferson Avenue stop in Bushwick. I rate Williamsburg over the others because it draws a diverse crowd midweek, has a more interesting bar scene (in my opinion), and you can get drunk for next to nothing on beer and shot specials.

As for college-style bars, there are several good choices scattered around Manhattan. Many of these host $1 beer nights during the week or have late night happy hours that draw decent crowds depending on the night (covered later in this chapter). A good go-to are any of the bars run by the NYC Best Bars group (www.nycbestbar.com). The most well-known are **The 13th Step** in East Village and **Off the Wagon** in Greenwich. These frat-tastic establishments are scattered all around the city and are always good for drink deals and a crowd. Another famous college spot that always delivers is **Turtle Bay**.

Speakeasies

One of the coolest things about New York nightlife is probation-style speakeasies. Typically, these are secret cocktail bars hidden around town behind unmarked doors and inconspicuous shop fronts. They're not cheap, and most of them make better date spots than pick-up joints, but I strongly recommend you check out at least one of them on your visit. It's a great experience. These places are also well-known for having the best bespoke cocktails in the city, if not the world. My favorites are **Apothéke** in Chinatown, **Angel's Share** and **PDT** in East Village, **Back Room** in the LES (best for picking up) and **Bathtub Gin** in the Club District.

Latin Spots

As I mentioned, on weekends it's almost like every little neighborhood Latin restaurant in the city turns into a dance spot. It's like the cabaret laws don't count for Hispanics. Dancing is in their blood. Most of these venues are pokey little dives with plastic chairs, cheesy music, and stumpy middle-aged Mexican fuglies who speak little or no English. Whereas Uptown and in Queens it's the polar opposite: pretentious lounges charging for admission and table service, where you'll see some of the sexiest Latinas alive. Luckily, there are also places that provide a happy median. If you want the full Latin experience, **Dyckman Street** is a good option. Another area you'll hear about is Jackson Heights, but I must warn you that most of these places are *bailaderos* (see **Queens** section). Aside from that, I urge you to be open-minded about your local Latin hang-outs. You'd be surprised at how much fun they can be and the quality of the ass you can grind.

Hookah Lounges

Astoria and Uptown are plagued with so-called 'hookah lounges' that effectively double as small dance clubs, with hip-hop being the music of choice. Most of these lounges are table service focused and lack a dance floor (although that doesn't stop girls from twerking), and tend to be very popular with non-whites who want to do the Models and Bottles thing without dropping a small fortune. These places attract good-looking, well-dressed women, but they tend to be in groups, and most of these places charge at the door. They are not ideal for picking up, but there are exceptions like **Le Souk** in Greenwich and **Katra** in Bowery.

Rock Bars

NYC has plenty of dive bars, but very few of them are what I would call true rock bars. I'm a big fan of rock bars, but as a Manhattanite, I find my options to be severely limited. Check out

Iron Horse if you're downtown or **Double Down Saloon** in East Village. Brooklyn has a lot more options. In Williamsburg, my favorite spots are **Rocka Rolla**, followed by **the Levee**. In Bushwick, there's the **Cobra Club**.

Rooftop Bars

New Yorkers are obsessed with rooftop bars. There are hundreds in the city. Sadly, most are ridiculously overpriced and are either boring lounges that cater to 30 to 40-something professionals or pretentious guest list/bottle service clubs. The latter rely on promoters to bring a ton of good-looking girls, but they're usually sectioned off at their respective tables, making it a less-than-ideal environment for picking up. There are some exceptions, but I tend to only recommend rooftop bars for either dates or to take in the skyline. Like visiting a speakeasy, I recommend you to go to at least one while you're in town. For the best views, I recommend **230 Fifth Rooftop** or the rotating restaurant **The View**. For a party, the best experience I've had is at **The Attic** and **PH-D**.

Themed Bars

If you want something a little different and don't want to blow your budget on speakeasies and rooftops, New York also has a couple of interesting themed bars worth checking out. For an Island vibe, there's **Tropical 128** nightclub, **Reunion Surf Bar**, and **Otto's Shrunken Head**. For a pirate theme—complete with stripper poles—there's **Wicked Willy's.** For a Bulgarian ski lodge vibe with a dance floor, I recommend **Mehanata**. If y'all want a redneck feel, grab a drink at **Trailer Park**, ride the mechanical bull at lively **Johnny Utah's**, or check out a honky-tonk band at **Skinny Dennis**. If you want bar girls line-dancing on the counter, there's **Coyote Ugly** (Hogs and Heifers is now closed). If you're around for Christmas, check out the pop-up bar **Miracle on 9th Street**. For something really corny, eat sushi at **Ninja** in Tribeca.

Bars with Live Music

I'm not talking about live music venues; I'm talking about venues with live music. In other words, not a place where people are there for the band, but where the band is there for the people. You want to be in a spot where the girls are there to socialize—and the music is just for atmosphere. Several spots fit the bill. **The Wayland** in Alphabet City gets my first pick. In Greenwich, there's **Red Lion** (pricey, but packed on weekends) and **Fat Cat** if you like the sound of Jazz and ping-pong tables. For something a little more alternative, I again recommend **Skinny Dennis** in Williamsburg. In LES, there's **Fat Baby** and **Pianos**. On the UWS and UES, there's **Prohibition** and **Session 73**, respectfully. Further Uptown, I'm a big fan of **Shrine** and **Silvana**.

Dance Clubs

As I've explained, the dance scene in New York is a little lacking. This is best exemplified by the fact that almost no genuine dance clubs exist in Manhattan north of Midtown. Leaving aside pretentious bottle service venues, if girls want to dance, they're usually restricted to either tiny dance floors or annoying mega-clubs. Very few dance venues provide a good balance of size, price, and atmosphere.

If you're looking for a big night out, the biggest clubs in the city are **Webster Hall** and the Ibiza club **Pacha**. Go online for discount tickets. Personally, I prefer Webster Hall, as it's more laid-back and reasonable. If you're in Williamsburg, check out **Output**. If you're in East Village, check out the back rooms of **Pourhouse** and **Bar None**. Westwards, **The Park** provides an excellent alternative to the strict doors of Meatpacking. However, my favorite area for dancing is the laid-back Lower East Side. Some of my top picks there are **The Delancey**, **Fat Baby,** and **Pianos.**

Models and Bottles (High-End Nightclubs)

Once you move into the Meatpacking District and southwest Chelsea, you enter the pretentious world of models and bottles. You find these type of places scattered all over NYC, but there's nothing quite like Meatpacking. Unfortunately, these places are also where you'll also find the most cocktail dresses, high heels, and the best-looking women. Getting in the doors of some of these places are often borderline-impossible, and some require to max out your credit card, but the sex ratio and quality of women you'll have access to will be unbeatable. So what's a man to do?

How to hack high-end clubs

If you're only in New York for a short time, don't know any promoters, and want to experience the high life, you basically have two options.

You can show up at the door with no vagina, in which case you'll be either refused point blank or asked to drop a couple hundred for bottle service. Then you'll be escorted to a lonely corner, far away from all the beautiful women, but close enough so you can see them huddling around some douchebag promoter's table, eagerly extending their glasses as he pops bottles and pours them free drinks, all of which are effectively subsidized by your sorry ass. While you're worried about checking your bank account, his only concern is which chick he's going to bang after he lures her into the bathroom for a line of coke.

Alternately, this sad scene can be avoided. If you go on off-peak nights, arrive before midnight, and have a hot piece of ass on your arm, you should have no trouble getting through the door. Just make sure that there're more girls than guys in your party, and make sure they're good-looking and wearing heels. Bouncers will straight up refuse your group if there's an ugly duckling in the bunch. It's an unfortunate paradox, but in NYC you need to be rolling with hotties to gain access to other hotties. You have to have chips on the table if you want to have a chance at the pot. It's also worth noting that sometimes clubs will let the girls in your group in for free, but still try and hustle the guys for a handout. It's annoying, and often you can talk your way out of it, but remember it's still a fraction of the cost compared to the alternative.

For those who are in New York for an extended period, I suggest getting in with a promoter. Not all of them are insufferable wankers, and the advantages are worth it. I've eaten at five-star restaurants and gotten bottle service at some of the most exclusive clubs in the city, where I drank with models, strippers, and socialites, and I never paid a penny for any of it. How did I get the hookup? By hanging out with attractive women. Clubs want cash and men want to hook up with hot women, so clubs use promoters as middle-men to bring the product to market. Top-tier females are in high demand and short supply in New York City, so promoters are desperate to get them in the door. Aside from incentivizing them with a table at a slick club and free drinks, they'll even let them bring a guy friend or two along, provided they're cool and the ratios work out. So befriend attractive women and network. The whole scene can be a little soulless and superficial, but at the end of the day, you'll have access to some of the best pussy on the planet.

PARTYING MIDWEEK

Finding a party midweek can be a chore. The East Village, Lower Manhattan, and Uptown barely have a pulse, so you're better off going out in LES, Williamsburg, Greenwich, or Meatpacking. Even then, I suggest you set your expectations low... *really* low. That way you won't be disappointed.

Below is a list of day-by-day recommendations if you're looking for crowds, or just want to get obliterated drunk for less than $20. I've also included a list of reliable venues that are good pretty much any night of the week, and I've excluded most places that require more than $100 for you to get through the door (researching all these places every night of the week was not viable).

Sunday

During the day, the party starts early at **Skinny Dennis** in Williamsburg with cheap beers and live music from 4 p.m. onwards. In the summer, there's also the infamous **Mr. Sunday** down by Sunset Park (google for more info). From there, you can either party in Williamsburg and head back to the city.

If you're in the city, I recommend you start in Chinatown. Fill up on cheap beer and oriental grub around Mott Street and then enjoy a cocktail and some chill live music at speakeasy **Apotheke**. After there, take a 10-minute walk up to **GoldBar** for hip-hop and high heels (free in, but it's hit or miss). If you want to split up the journey, there's an optional stop-off in **the Mulberry Project** in Little Italy (it will be completely dead, but it's another hidden another speakeasy). Better yet, skip GoldBar and go to **Pianos** in LES.

If you're looking for something higher-end, it's models and hip-hop night at **Electric Room** in the Meatpacking District. You'll need to have a beaut on your arm to get in, though.

Monday

On Monday nights, most people out partying are either students, tourists, or those in the service industry. Most of the action happens west of Broadway.

For a well-balanced night, there's always a good crowd for cheap beers at **Off The Wagon**. I suggest setting up camp here, but if you get bored, take a quick pit stop at **Wicked Willy's** for some cheap tequila shots and a look around, then go across the road and head upstairs to **Le Souk** for their notorious 'Twerk Night'. The party there doesn't get going there till after 1 a.m., but the earlier you go, the less likely you'll have to pay in if you're a single male. It's a little pretentious, but it has some of the most diverse and best-looking ladies you'll find in the city.

In LES, start off with live music in **Back Room** before hitting up upstairs at **Pianos**.

Monday is also a big night for several Meatpacking spots. **PH-D** is the go-to spot for the young and beautiful from about 11 p.m. to 2 a.m., but you'll be asked for $100 bar minimum per person. That may sound expensive, but at **Avenue** they'll be looking for $250 per person, and **Catch Rooftop** will quote you $1000+ for a table. On the other end of the spectrum, **Cielo** charges $20 in for their 'deep space' party, but it's poorly attended and the crowd is pretty ugly. A good compromise is hip-hop night at **The Griffin,** which charge around $60 for general admission.

On the Upper West and East Sides, **Jake's Dilemma** and **The Stumble Inn** offer $1 beers and a college crowd. In Williamsburg, **Skinny Dennis** attracts a crowd as always.

In East Village, **Mona's** hosts a popular Bluegrass night.

Tuesday

Many consider Tuesday night the quietest night of the week. Options are very limited, but personally, I find them better than those on Mondays.

On the East Side, things kick off with Haitian *Kompa* night at **Katra** in the Lower East Side. The party hits full swing around ten o'clock and ends a little after midnight, so get here around nine o'clock. From here, head north to **The 13th Step** for dollar beers and college girls. The sex ratio can be a bit iffy, but there's still plenty of girls and it's arguably the best party you'll find on a Tuesday.

Farther north, there's also $1 beers at **McFadden's**.

In Greenwich, it's college night for NYU at **Off the Wagon** and **Le Souk** also draws a crowd.

In Brooklyn, if you like reggae, check out **Bembe.**

In Meatpacking, **1Oak** and **Avenue** are popping.

Wednesdays

Wednesday nights are a popular night for college students.

In Midtown East, there's $1 beers and a big party at **Turtle Bay**. This is probably your best option.

The Upper West Side also comes to life as Columbia students venture out for student night. It's the only night I bother going out in the area. Senior nights at **Bernard and Swartz** attracts the largest crowd, followed by **1020**. There's also dollar beers at nearby **Lion's Head.** It's best to go early as these places empty out by 2 a.m.

In Greenwich, there're $1 beers at **Down the Hatch** and half price off everything at **Off the Wagon**.

In East Village and LES, there're $8 pitchers at **Hair of the Dog,** and as always **Pianos** draws the dance crowd.

On the higher end of things, it's a big night for **Marquee** in Chelsea. It's also a decent night for several clubs in Meatpacking, such as **Cielo** and **Le Bain**.

A pub crawl in Williamsburg is also a good option for Wednesdays.

Thursdays

There are plenty of good options on Thursday nights. It's one of the most popular nights of the week to go out, and a lot of places are well attended.

To pregame with cheap beer and a decent party, head to Midtown East. There're $1 beer mugs and free mechanic bull rides for 'College Rodeo Night' at **Johnny Utah's**, and nearby **Turtle Bay** offer an open bar for just $20. Both deals stop at 1 a.m.

From there, if you're looking for something higher end, it's a big night for **Lavo** nearby. However, I recommend hitting up the LES if you want something more laid-back. The area around **Ludlow St.** and **Stanton St.** is buzzing.

Williamsburg is also good on Thursdays when many weekend dance spots such as **Output** open their doors. **Union Pool** is busy too.

List of Reliable Venues

In addition to the venues mentioned above, here is a short list of places I've found to be consistently busy or fun most nights. If you know of any you feel should be added to this list, please e-mail me at thenaughtynomad@gmail.com or tweet me @naughtynomad.

- ❖ **Pianos,** Lower East Side (dancing)
- ❖ **The Mean Fiddler**, Midtown West (dancing)
- ❖ **Turtle Bay**, Midtown East (dancing)
- ❖ **The Meatpacking District** (in general)
- ❖ **Rudy's**, Midtown West (pregame spot before Fiddler)
- ❖ **Off the Wagon,** Greenwich
- ❖ **Le Souk,** Greenwich
- ❖ **Bathtub Gin,** Club District (speakeasy)
- ❖ **Employee's Only,** West Village (speakeasy)
- ❖ **Back Room,** Lower East Side (speakeasy)

- ❖ **The Wayland**, East Village (early)
- ❖ **Silvana**, Harlem (dancing)
- ❖ **Shrine**, Harlem (dancing)
- ❖ **Union Pool,** Williamsburg
- ❖ **Skinny Dennis**, Williamsburg
- ❖ **The Levee**, Williamsburg

THE DRUG SCENE

New Yorkers love drugs. I can think of few cities where the casual use of hard drugs is so commonplace and blasé. Even for all my worldly experience, New York still popped several cherries of mine when it came to drugs. I've always hated the idea of cocaine (I still don't like it), but when a stripper picks you up in a limo and tells you to take a bump off her stomach, you just fucking do it. Similarly, when you get offered free drugs that are extremely hard to come across, such as acid or DMT, the opportunity is a little hard to pass up.

The most popular drugs in NYC are weed, molly, and cocaine. You can find these from most street dealers.

Marijuana

It seems like almost everybody smokes weed here. Even on the busy streets of Midtown, it's not uncommon to catch a whiff of the stuff. Scoring a dime bag is so easy and convenient it's like popping into the deli for a sandwich.

In built-up areas like Upper Manhattan, for example, two or more dealers set up shop in set locations (building entrances, street corners, in front of delis or bars etc.) and rotate shifts, working around the clock from the late afternoon through to when the bars close. Many of these guys also have access to harder drugs. If you can't find these corner boys, just ask young people around the neighborhood and you'll get pointed in the right direction. Expect to get around half a gram for $10.

In the boroughs, things work a little differently. Because there's often not enough street traffic to justify hanging out on a corner, a lot of dealers communicate by phone and deal with referrals from friends and acquaintances. Due to the nature of this selling method, these dealers normally require you to buy more product when purchasing (usually bags worth $30-50+). This may discourage the short-term visitor, but the good news is most of these guys have cars and will even deliver. Again, talking to people is the only way to get sorted. For obvious reasons, I cannot publish any locations or contact details for dealers.

Cocaine

Cocaine is very popular in the city. This is especially true among the most attractive of women, who inevitably become exposed to it as they swim up to higher social circles. Models, dancers, and hired guns are particularly vulnerable to getting hooked on the stuff. They come to the city swearing they'd never touch it, but then they get too fucked up one night and cave when offered their first bump, and the next thing you know they're hooking up with their hookup and scoring blow for blowjobs. I wish I were exaggerating, but I've seen it happen. I've even lost potential bangs to lesser men purely because there was coke on offer. An example from a word-for-word text conversation:

Her: "Wanna fuck tonight?"
Me: "Hmm…I should be free around midnight."
Her: "Do you do blow?"
Me: "Not my style."
Her: "Too bad."

As you can guess, the bitch moved on to the next guy on the line, literally and figuratively. As I said, it's not for me, but if you do blow yourself, you'll find it reliable bait for many women in NYC. You can buy coke from most street dealers. They typically sell $40 bags containing a little over half a gram.

Molly (MDMA)

When I first arrived in America, everybody I talked to seemed to be buzzing about this drug called 'molly.' It's basically MDMA, a purer version of ecstasy. It usually comes in a crystalline form that you can break up into a powder and dissolve in liquid. Similar to ecstasy, you experience feelings of euphoria, unbounded love and energy, and the compulsive need to gnaw your tongue till your jaw falls off. However, unlike ecstasy, the 'scag' effect and desire to die the next day isn't nearly as bad. The cost is usually $30-40 for around 100mg (a hefty dose for a first-time user).

Know the risks

The NYPD's new stop-and-frisk policy means you can be searched at any officer's behest if they regard you as suspicious. They can also search you for any small violation or misdemeanor (such as drinking on the street or hopping a turnstile.) Unsurprisingly, the darker your skin, the more likely you are to be searched. In 2014, nearly 90% of those searched were either Black or Latino.

For a first-time offender, possession of up to 25 grams of marijuana is a slap on the wrist, punishable by a fine of $100. For cocaine, molly, or any other hard drugs, it's all about the weight. If you only have a small amount (less than half a gram of coke or 25mg of MDMA), it's considered a Class A misdemeanor. If it's your first offence, you may get away with a plea for disorderly conduct. This requires you to pay a sizable fine, but, pending good behavior, your case should eventually be sealed and you won't have a criminal record. However, if you get caught with more than that—let's say a gram—and you're looking at a Class D felony, punishable by up to one year in jail as well as a minimum fine of $1,000. With a bit of luck and a good lawyer, you'll be able to avoid any jail time with probation, but you'll have a public record.

Neighborhood Map of NYC

1. Lower Manhattan
2. Greenwich & Clubs
3. East Village & LES
4. Midtown West
5. Midtown East
6. Upper West Side
7. Upper East Side
8. Upper Manhatten
9. Queens
10. Brooklyn

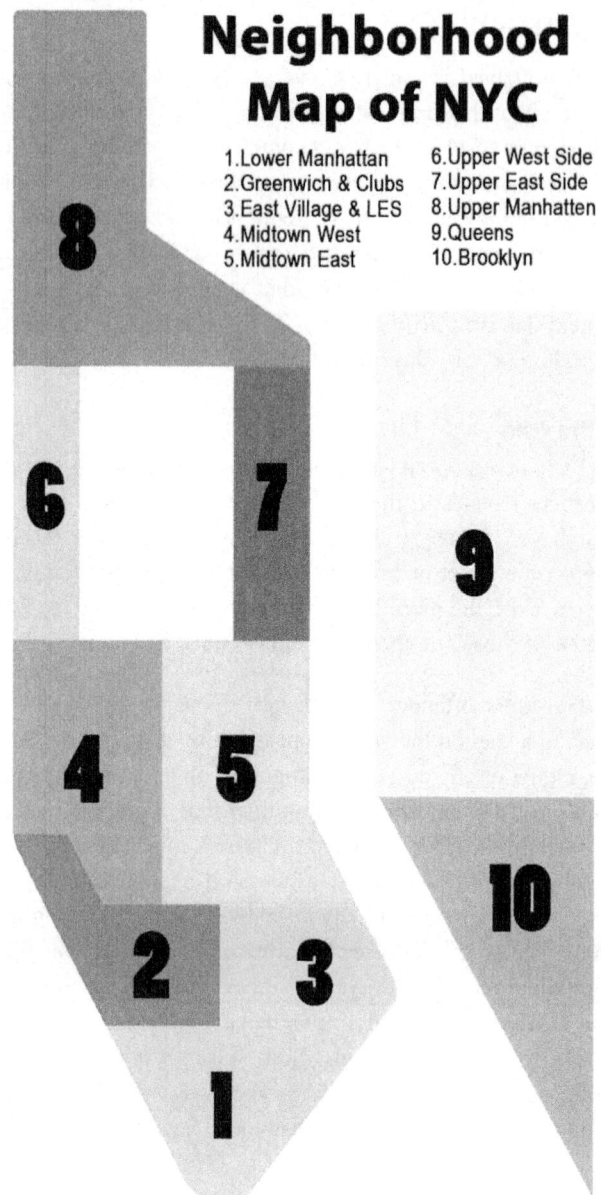

NEIGHBORHOOD OVERVIEW

1. LOWER MANHATTAN

From the maze of the Financial District to vibrant Chinatown, to the famous 'hoods of Little Italy, SoHo, and Tribeca: nowhere in the city will you find greater contrast. Nightlife is sparse in the area, but there are a few hidden gems about.

2. GREENWICH VILLAGE & CLUB DISTRICT

The best part of town to experience the full spectrum of New York nightlife. With NYU at its heart and the velvet ropes of the Meatpacking District to the west, you can pay $1 for a beer in one place and drop 2K for a table service in the next.

3. EAST VILLAGE & LOWER EAST SIDE (LES)

The east side is the no.1 choice for 'real' New Yorkers when it comes to nightlife, particularly the Lower East Side. Options here are vast, with everything from speakeasies to rock bars to mega-clubs. Think Williamsburg with better-looking women.

4. MIDTOWN WEST

Chelsea, Hell's Kitchen, and Times Square are better known for gay bars, restaurants, and tourist traps, but north of 42nd is always buzzing and has some of the best pubs and clubs in the city. It's a great place for a messy pub crawl.

5. MIDTOWN EAST

A cluster-fuck of residential and commercial 'hoods, this area of the city is pretty boring, but there're a few rooftop bars and great midweek party spots that are worth the trip.

6. UPPER WEST SIDE (UWS)

A subdued neighborhood that's best avoided. The area around Columbia University can be decent Wed-Sat during the school term, but otherwise, there are few reasons to venture here unless you're staying in the area or farther north.

7. UPPER EAST SIDE (UES)

The wealthiest area of the city, mainly inhibited by old rich white people, but things are changing. Single females now outnumber males nearly 2-to-1, and the nightlife is improving. On weekends it's the ideal place for picking up top-tier white chicks if you don't want to deal with Meatpacking.

8. HARLEM & ABOVE

Rapidly changing and dynamic, a night out in Harlem and Upper Manhattan is always interesting. Hipsters have invaded West Harlem, but the French African influence in Central Harlem and the Latin vibes of the Heights have spawned some great nightlife. If you like African and Hispanic women, look no further.

9. QUEENS

Officially the most ethnically diverse place on planet earth. Overall, the nightlife is sparse, needlessly pretentious, and often leaves you scratching your head, but there are places worth exploring if you end up moving here.

10. BROOKLYN

Is Williamsburg the coolest nightlife area in all of New York? It could well be. And its younger brother Bushwick might be even *cooler*. BK is a mecca for unpretentious nightlife.

Lower Manhattan

At the southern tip of the island lies Lower Manhattan, the historical core of the city. For me, the maze of the Financial District (FiDi) and the otherworldly feel of Chinatown give it more character and charm than anywhere else on the island. However, when it comes to partying and picking up, it's like double D's on a fat chick; it's just not worth it, bro. Decent nightlife options are scarce and sparsely located, but there are some amazing spots you don't want to miss.

Be sure to visit my favorite little side street in all of New York: Doyers Street in Chinatown (also known as Murder's Alley). It looks like the corner of some Beijing slum, but it has many secrets. Pregame with some cheap bottles of Tsingtao and then head here to indulge in a cocktail at hidden speakeasy **Apothéke.** After that, mosey next door to underground **Pulqueria** for salsa dancing Latinas. Chinatown also hosts major party spots **La Baron** and **Santos Party House**—although I prefer the less pretentious dance scene in nearby LES.

If you're in FiDi, consider a pub crawl on the infamous bar strip of **Stone Street** with a side-visit to nearby **The Dead Rabbit**: voted the best bar in the world in 2015. If you're looking for something a bit wilder or wanna pregame, do a cheap shot and beer combo and hit on some trashy rock chicks at **The Iron Horse**.

Tribeca and SoHo and pretty uninspiring for nightlife. There's a little bit of action on the side streets along Canal Street, the best of a bad lot being **M 1-5 Lounge.**

Around Little Italy, you can also do a little speakeasy tour by visiting **The Mulberry Project**, **The Ship**, and **Pravda** (Russian). For girls, there are uppity clubs **GoldBar** and **Southside**: outlining orbiters of the action of the Lower East Side.

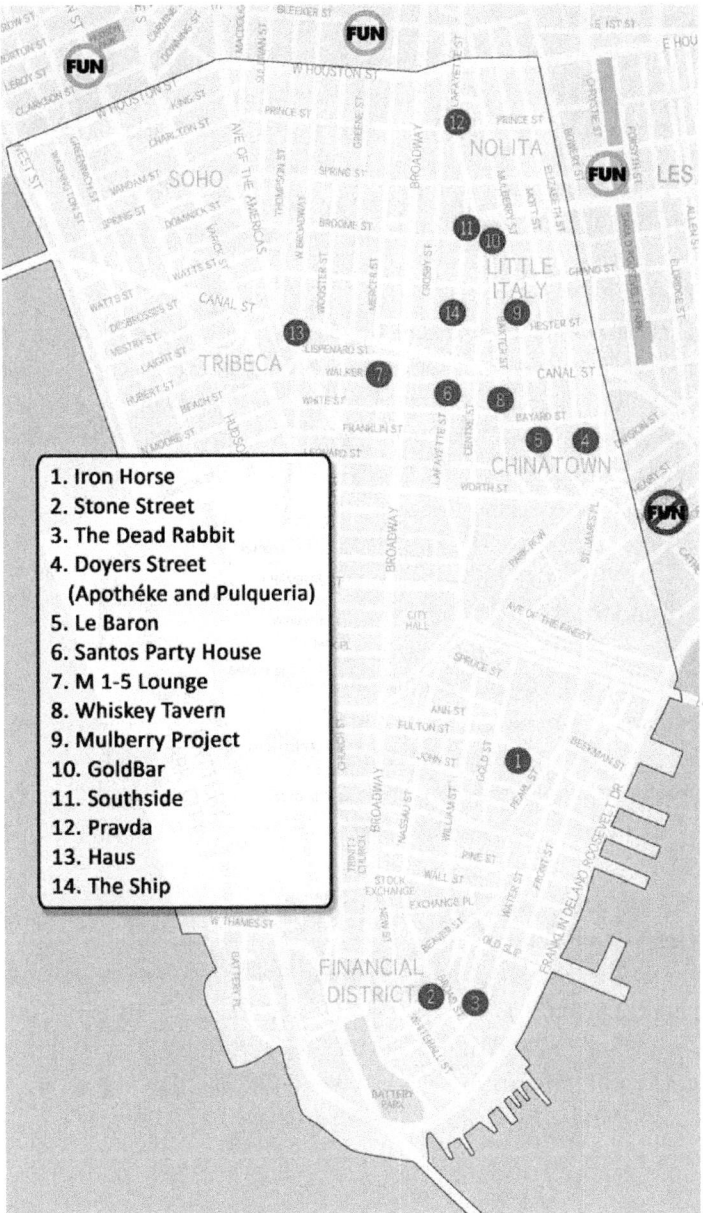

1. Iron Horse
2. Stone Street
3. The Dead Rabbit
4. Doyers Street
   (Apothéke and Pulqueria)
5. Le Baron
6. Santos Party House
7. M 1-5 Lounge
8. Whiskey Tavern
9. Mulberry Project
10. GoldBar
11. Southside
12. Pravda
13. Haus
14. The Ship

Area Profile
Population: 152k
Age: 34 is the average, 37% aged between 20 and 35.
Race: 72% White, 15% Asian, 8% Hispanic, 2% Black, 3% other.

Financial District (FiDi)

The Iron Horse   Rock Bar, Dive Bar

This heavy-metal version of Coyote Ugly is one of Manhattan's coolest dive bars, with rock chicks serving cheap drinks, a wheel of death, pool table, counter-top dancing, and swings above the bar. It was a bit of a sausage fest when I checked it out, but the whole concept along with Marilyn Manson playlist left me with a favorable impression. It's easily the coolest bar in FiDi for me. ⌂ *ironhorsenyc.com; 646-546-5426; 32 Cliff St.; till 4 AM.*

Stone Street   Bar Strip

This small cobblestone street in the heart of FiDi is great for a pub crawl because it's the only thing resembling a genuine bar strip in the city. It's particular vibrant in the summertime when the street becomes one giant beer garden. There's more of an after-work crowd, but the largest bar, **Ulysses**, keeps the party going till 4 a.m. every night. ⌂ *ulyssesnyc.com; 212-482-0400; Stone St.; till 4 AM.*

The Dead Rabbit   Cocktail Bar

A much-loved old-school cocktail bar spread over two floors. The industry voted it the best bar in the world in 2015, so that alone should sell it. Upstairs is arguably the best place for serious drinking in the area. It's not much of a pick-up place, however. ⌂ *deadrabbitnyc.com; 646-422-7906; 30 Water St.; till 4 AM.*

Chinatown

Apothéke Speakeasy, TOP PICK!

Hidden down a quiet grimy side street in Chinatown, through an unmarked door under a sign reading 'chemist', you'll find one of the coolest speakeasies on the planet. A cross between a chemistry lab and a 19th century Parisian Absinthe den, this place is a must if you're downtown. It's pricey ($15 a cocktail), but the drinks are incredible, the girls are good-looking, and it draws a crowd seven nights a week. It's great for both a date or a stop-off on a night out. Between 9 p.m. and 11 p.m. it can get a little packed, and the door is stricter. Try to arrive around midnight. There's live music on Wednesdays and Sundays. △ *apothekenyc.com; 212-406-0400; 9 Doyers St.; till 2 AM.*

Pulqueria Latin, Live Music, Dance Club, TOP PICK!

Owned by the same people behind Apothéke next door, this large underground Mexican restaurant turns into a cool little dancing spot late night on weekends. They also have DJs midweek and live salsa music on Wednesdays. Monday is industry night and there's happy hour all night. The only downside about this place is that things wrap up relatively early. △ *pulquerianyc.com; 212-227-3099; 11 Doyers St.; Mon-Thurs till 12 PM, Fri & Sat till 2 AM.*

La Baron Dance Club

Formally an upmarket brothel, this well-known pretentious French club has several pokey rooms over three floors. The crowd comes late and are mainly European, especially French. The door can be tough. It's better to visit on a weekday—preferably with a cute female—and only worth a visit if you happen to be visiting nearby Doyers Street. △ *lebaronnyc.com; 212-962-2545; 32 Mulberry St.; Tues-Sat till 4 AM.*

Santos Party House Dance Club, Live Music

This venue is events driven, so check online to see what's going on. There's big name DJs and a big dance crowd, but drinks are pricey, and there's usually a $20 admission (discounted tickets available online). If that doesn't sound appealing, nearby M 1-5 Lounge is usually free in. ⌂ *santospartyhouse.com; 212-584-5492; 96 Lafayette St.; Fri & Sat till 4 AM.*

Whiskey Tavern Bar

One of the only 'normal' bars in the area, it's popular with 20-to-30 somethings and very busy on weekends. There's a $10 beer and shot combo available if you're looking for a pit stop. ⌂ *whiskeytavernnyc.com; 212-374-9119; 79 Baxter St.; till 4 AM.*

Wo Hop Chinese Restaurant

A grubby-looking subterranean Chinese restaurant that I'm only mentioning because it's open 24 hours and good for beers at 5 a.m. Cash only. ⌂ *wohopnyc.com; 212-962-8617; 17 Mott St.; 24 hours.*

Little Italy & Nolita
(Nolita is short for North of Little Italy)

The Mulberry Project Speakeasy, Date Spot

A tiny underground speakeasy in the heart of Little Italy. The crowd is less consistent than other speakeasies, but it's good for late evenings and on weekends. ⌂ *mulberryproject.com; 646-448-4536; 149 Mulberry St.; Thurs-Sun till 2 AM, Fri &Sat till 4 AM.*

Pravda Speakeasy, Date Spot, Themed Bar

An inconspicuous, underground Russian cocktail bar that's atmospheric, dimly-lit, and a great place for a quiet drink. Try the infused vodkas. ⌂ *pravdany.com; 212-226-4944; 281 Lafayette St.; Sun & Mon till 12 AM, Tues-Thurs till 1 AM, Fri & Sat till 3 AM .*

GoldBar Lounge, Dance Club, Models and Bottles

A long narrow venue with overpriced drinks and table service. It's not my style, but it can be good for a party on Sunday night when there's free entry and sexy girls grinding to hip-hop. Recently, the crowd has been hit or miss, but if you like to smoke weed indoors, let's just say this place is 'non-judgmental.' ⌂ *goldbarnewyork.com; 212-274-1568; 389 Broome St.; Thurs-Sun till 4 AM.*

Southside Dance Club

An alternative to GoldBar, this small basement club has a young, attractive crowd, a tough door, and overpriced drinks. It's meatpacking in Nolita. ⌂ *nycsouthside.com; 212-680-5601; 2 Cleveland Pl.; Wed-Sat till 4 AM.*

Tribeca & SoHo
*(Short for **Tri**angle **be**low **Ca**nal St. and **South** of **Hou**ston St.)*

M 1-5 Lounge Dance Club

More of a dance club than a lounge, this spacious room centers around a huge circular bar and attracts a diverse young crowd on weekends that come to dance to chart music. There's no cover or dress code, and the lack of seating makes it ideal for approaching. The vibe is good, but attendance numbers are a little inconsistent. If you're in the area after midnight, definitely stick your head in. ⌂ *m1-5.com; 212-965-1701; 52 Walker St,; till 4 AM.*

Haus Lounge, Dance Club

A three-floor venue that is more of a noisy bottle service lounge than a dance club. Expect to drop about $20-30 for admission, pay $9 for bottled beer, and not have anywhere to dance. The only upside is that there're lots of good-looking young girls, and the door is easier than its meatpacking counterparts. ⌂ *haus-nyc.com; 917-282-1800; 285 West Broadway.; Thurs-Sat till 4 AM.*

The Ship <small>Speakeasy, Themed Bar</small>

Brought to you by the same people behind PDT, this nautical-themed cocktail bar is hidden behind metal doors. It's a good date spot or stop-off on a crawl. ⌂ *theshipnyc.com; number; 158 Lafayette St.; Mon-Wed till 1 AM, Thurs-Sat till 3 AM.*

Greenwich Village and the Club District

From college dive bars to exclusive high-end clubs, live music venues to cocktail bars, and comedy clubs to beer halls, no part of town better exemplifies the full spectrum of NYC nightlife. The LES and Williamsburg may have more street cred nowadays, but nowhere has a higher concentration of bars or beautiful women than here.

New Yorkers tend to divide this part of town into three parts. Some describe the whole area as Greenwich, but locals only use that term when referring to the area around NYU, whereas 'West Village' is employed for the anything west of 6th Ave. Then there's the tiny northwest enclave known as the Meatpacking District, an area synonymous with clubbing and high-end nightlife. The scene here spills north past 14th street into Chelsea, but for New Yorkers is all part of the same beast. For the rest of this section, I simply refer to that whole area as the Club District.

Around NYU, most of the action centers around Bleecker St. and MacDougal St. This area is bustling with students, artsy types, and tourists. Make reservations at **The Comedy Cellar** for the best possible start to a night out in NYC. Midweek check out **Off the Wagon** for cheap booze and college girls. For high-heeled minorities and hip-hop, there's **Le Souk**. On weekends hit up Bleecker Street. **Red Lion** is good for live music, but if DJs and stripper poles are more your scene, pop into **Wicked Willy's** next door. There's also **Fat Black Pussycat** for darker women.

Moving into the quieter neighborhood of West Village, subterranean games-center **Fat Cat** offers everything ping-pong to live jazz. Check out speakeasy **Employees Only** for cocktails and a midweek crowd. Late on weekends the best place to pick up is **Fiddlesticks** (a favorite haunt of mine).

North of West Village, you'll find yourself on the cobblestone streets of the Meatpacking District. Here the skirts get shorter and prices double. You haven't a hope of getting into most of these places unless you either know a promoter, drop a bomb for a table reservation, or show suited up with a model on your arm. However, there are a few exceptions. Be sure to check out coffee shop speakeasy **Bathtub Gin**. Other popular drinking spots are **Brass Monkey** and **The Standard Biergarten**. End your night at **The Park Nightclub**. If you can get in, I also recommend **The Jane Hotel, Le Bain,** and **PH-D Rooftop.**

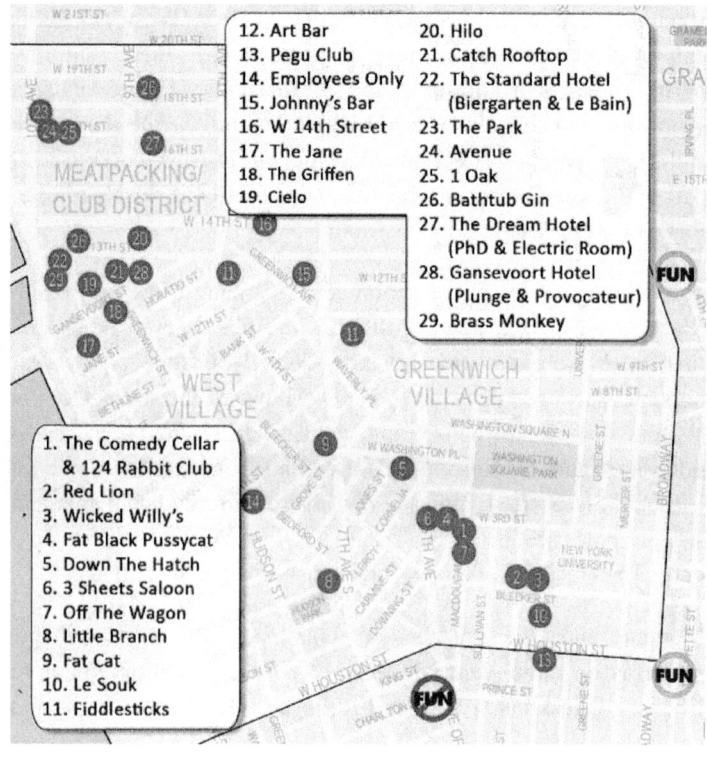

12. Art Bar
13. Pegu Club
14. Employees Only
15. Johnny's Bar
16. W 14th Street
17. The Jane
18. The Griffen
19. Cielo
20. Hilo
21. Catch Rooftop
22. The Standard Hotel
    (Biergarten & Le Bain)
23. The Park
24. Avenue
25. 1 Oak
26. Bathtub Gin
27. The Dream Hotel
    (PhD & Electric Room)
28. Gansevoort Hotel
    (Plunge & Provocateur)
29. Brass Monkey

1. The Comedy Cellar
   & 124 Rabbit Club
2. Red Lion
3. Wicked Willy's
4. Fat Black Pussycat
5. Down The Hatch
6. 3 Sheets Saloon
7. Off The Wagon
8. Little Branch
9. Fat Cat
10. Le Souk
11. Fiddlesticks

Area Profile (excluding Southeast Chelsea)
Population: 72k
Average Age: 36, with roughly 20% aged between 20 and 35.
Race: 79% White, 9% Asian, 6% Hispanic, 2% Black, 4% other.

Around NYU

The Comedy Cellar ^{TOP PICK!}

I can't recommend this place highly enough. It's pokey size is perfect for comedy gigs, the atmosphere is electric, and tickets and beer pitchers are reasonably priced. The standard is also world-class, with famous names often dropping by. With up to six shows a night, there's no excuse to miss this spot. It's the best possible start to a night out in the city. Make sure you reserve online beforehand. ⌂ *comedycellar.com; 213-251-3480; 117 MacDougal Street; last show is at 11.15 PM weekdays and 12.15 AM weekends.*

Off the Wagon, 3 Sheets Saloon, and Down the Hatch ^{Dive Bar, College Spot}

Three locations, but basically the same bar. Brought to by the same people behind The 13th Step, these frat bars are reliable for cheap beer, bar snacks, and lots of douchebags…but they're good for getting drunk on the cheap. Each of them rotates drink specials depending on the night, so look online for the best deals. Off The Wagon is the most consistent for a crowd and attracts the most women. ⌂ *nycbestbar.com; see map for locations; till 4 AM.*

124 Old Rabbit Club ^{Dive Bar, Speakeasy}

A secretive bomb-shelter dive bar hidden underground, speakeasy style. It's tiny, so it's not a place to pick up, but people seem to love it because it's quiet and a nice change from the frat bars. Cash only. ⌂ *212-254-0575; 124 MacDougal St.; Sun-Thurs till 2 AM, Fri & Sat till 4 AM.*

Wicked Willy's Themed Bar, Dive Bar, College Spot

A long pirate-themed bar with beer pong tables, drink specials, and stripper poles. It can be pretty dead early in the week, but on weekends there's live music and a good party vibe. △ *wickedwillys.com; 212-254-8592; 149 Bleecker St.; till 4 AM.*

Pegu Club Cocktail Bar, Date Spot

Being on the south side of Houston Street technically makes this a SoHo joint, but I've included it here because it's only one block from Bleecker St. and one of the only half-decent date spots around NYU. △ *peguclub.com; 212-473-7348; 77 W Houston St.; Thurs-Sun, till 4 AM.*

Le Souk Lounge Hookah Lounge, Dance Club

A high-end Moroccan hookah lounge with a lot of table service, a tiny dance area, and an extremely ethnically diverse crowd. It's a little cliquey because of the table layout, and not a place I'd usually recommend, but it attracts one of the sexiest crowds in the city. It also has the best party I've come across on a Monday night (twerk night). It's $7 for a bottled beer, so you may want to consider pregaming. They say there's a cover for guys after midnight, but I've always talked my way in for free. Dress sharp and say you're a tourist. △ *lesoukny.com; 212-777-5454; 510 LaGuardia Pl.; till 4 AM.*

The Fat Black Pussycat Disco Bar, Date Spot

A cool bar to pregame or bring a date. The main room has a pool table and darts. The crowd is a mix of Blacks and Whites. It's set up to cater for large groups, but late on weekends they have good DJs that compel people off their seats. In addition to the main room, there's a very sultry Moroccan-style lounge in the back that's perfect for a date. They also 50% off drinks if you went to a show at the Comedy Cellar next door. △ *thefatblackpussycat.com; 212-533-4790; 130 W. 3rd Street; till 4 AM.*

The Red Lion ^{Pub, Live Music}

It's overpriced, but there's three bands a night every night, and the music is on point. On weekends it can get a little crowded and there's a $10 cover, but it's a reliable place for a party. ⌂ *redlionnyc.com; 212-260-9797; 151 Bleecker St.; till 4 AM.*

West Village

Fiddlesticks ^{College Bar, TOP PICK!}

After midnight on weekends this pick-up joint is packed with good-looking young people. The crowd can be a little preppy, but there's a DJ and a great vibe in the place. I've consistently picked up here without much effort. Come early and try to get a place at the bar near the service station. It's quiet midweek, but it's only $5 for American beers, making it the cheapest place for a good pint in the area. ⌂ *fiddlesticksnyc.com; 212-463-0516; 56 Greenwich Ave; till 4 AM.*

Johnny's Bar ^{Dive Bar}

This tiny place is quite possibly the only legitimate dive bar in West Village. There are shot specials and the likes of Rolling Rock start at $3.50 a pint. It's a good place to pregame and also attracts female students on a budget. Cash only. ⌂ *johnnysbarnyc.com, 212-741-5279; 90 Greenwich Ave; till 4 AM.*

Art Bar ^{Dive Bar, Date Spot}

A low-key 'chic dive' with relatively cheap beer. The back room looks like an art collector's living room that was turned into storage space for second-hand furniture, but somehow the candlelight and fireplace ties the whole thing together. It's perfect for dates or a quiet pint. ⌂ *artbar.com; 212-727-0244; 52 8th Ave.; till 4 AM.*

Fat Cat <small>Dive Bar, Themed Bar, Live Music, Date Spot</small>

A large basement that has combines a pool hall and live jazz venue. There's also ping-pong tables, shuffleboard, and board games. It's a little bizarre and not the best place to mingle, but the beer is cheap, and it's a great place to hang out with friends. ⌂ *fatcatmusic.org; 212-675-6056; 75 Christopher St.; till 5 AM.*

Employee's Only <small>Speakeasy</small>

There is a fortune teller lady in the window and a sign saying 'Psychic', but go through the door and you'll find a lively little cocktail bar. Sadly, 'EO' has been a victim of its own success and now needs to post a permanent doorman out the front. It ruins the illusion, but this place is still packed every night, making it a top pick for West Village. ⌂ *employeesonlynyc.com; 212-242-3021; 510 Hudson Street (near Christopher St. Station).; till 4 AM.*

Little Branch <small>Speakeasy, Date Spot</small>

Behind an unmarked door, you'll find this cozy underground cocktail bar. It's a great date spot for in-the-know New Yorkers. ⌂ *212-929-4360; 20 7th Ave. St.; till 3 AM.*

W 14th Strip <small>Nightlife Strip</small>

Between 7th and 8th Avenue there's a handful of drinking spots ranging from laid-back dives like **Wood & Ales** and Brazilian hangout **The Girl From Ipanema** to uber-pretentious **Up & Down** where you pay 2k for a table. It's not a bad street to wonder down if you're looking for a stop-off, but don't go out of your way. ⌂ *West 14th St. (Btwn 7th and 8th Ave.); Most till 4 AM.*

Meatpacking & Around (Club District)

Bathtub Gin Speakeasy, TOP PICK!

This is one of NYC's coolest speakeasies and I'd highly recommend it any night of the week. Hidden behind the wall of an actual coffee shop, this prohibition style cocktail joint is a decent size and a lot livelier than other speakeasies, making it one of the few conducive for mingling. If you're planning on going there on the weekend, you may want to make a reservation. ⌂ *bathtubginnyc.com; 646-559-1671; 132 9th Ave.; Sun-Wed till 2 AM, Thurs-Sat till 4 AM.*

The Standard Biergarten Beer Garden

A massive outdoor German beer garden under the High Line. It's not cheap, and it gets ridiculously packed on weekends, but if you're here at the right time during the warmer months, it's the perfect place in the area to grab a stein and strike up a conversation. ⌂ *standardhotels.com; 212-645-4646; 848 Washington St.; Sun-Wed till 1 AM, Thurs-Sat till 2 AM.*

The Park Dance Club, Lounge, TOP PICK!

A welcome relief from the typical Club District bullshit. If you're a single guy looking to party, and you want to pick up on a Friday or Saturday, this place is a great option. Named after its former function as a parking garage, this gigantic space is like three venues in one, with a classy lounge and a two-story nightclub. It can feel a little sparse and slows down in the summer, but admission is free, pints are reasonably priced, and it has a diverse good-looking crowd. There are few venues in the city that offer a better compromise. During the school term, it also attracts a lot of smokin' Indian chicks. Dress smart. ⌂ *theparknyc.com; 212-352-3313; 118 10th Ave.; Fri & Sat till 4 AM.*

Brass Monkey ^{Bar, Rooftop}

An unpretentious tri-level bar with a rooftop terrace. There's no dance floor, and it can be very hit or miss with the crowd, but it's the only place in Meatpacking resembling a 'normal' bar, and it's not too loud for conversation. There can be a bit of a queue for the rooftop section; unfortunately, this is where most of the single women gravitate. ⌂ *brassmonkeynyc.com; 212-675-6686; 55 Little W 12th St.; till 4 AM..*

Plunge Rooftop Lounge ^{Rooftop Lounge}

A mediocre rooftop bar above the Gansevoort hotel. It's $10 for a beer and mainly table service, but it's not that difficult to gain entry. The best place to pick up is by the bar. The crowd is mainly European, but don't expect to see any models. ⌂ *gansevoorthotelgroup.com; 212-206-6700; 18 9th Ave.; till 4 AM.*

Ceilo ^{Dance Club}

One of the few places in meatpacking that's more dance floor than table service and also accessible to single males. It's also one of the few places where you can find a pulse on a Monday (but barely). That said, it's overrated and only worth checking out if you're absolutely fucked up. It's smaller than other dance clubs, the crowd ain't too pretty, and it's very overpriced. Expect to pay $20+ for admission (cheaper online), $8 for bottled beer, $6 for water, and be wary that a 20% gratuity is automatically added to every check. ⌂ *cieloclub.com; 646-543-8556; 18 Little W 12th St.; till 4 AM, closed Sun & Tues.*

HILO ^{Disco Bar, Dance Club}

Similar to Cielo, there's a $20 cover, but at least you know you're getting in. HILO is probably the least pretentious meatpacking club. The ladies may not look as good, but at least they're dancing and more laid-back. ⌂ *hilobarnyc.com; 212-837-4700; 26 9th Av.; Thurs-Sat till 4 AM..*

Le Bain Rooftop, Dance Club

At the top of the Standard is one of NYC's coolest rooftop clubs, with amazing views, and a young, good-looking international crowd. The door is super strict, but the vibe inside is surprisingly unpretentious. Avoid Tuesdays (gay night). The actual rooftop is also a great place to go during the day. ⌂ *standardhotels.com; 212-645-4646; 848 Washington St.; Wed-Sat till 4 AM, Sun till 3 AM.*

Electric Room Dance Club, Models and Bottles

Walk down the loading dock of the Dream Hotel and you'll find the entrance to this exclusive little basement club. This used to be the hardest door in the city, but things have gone downhill a little since its heyday. You still need to look cool and have a hottie on your arm to gain entry, but I've come here on a Friday after midnight and there was barely a line. It's not a bad spot for a late night party midweek (go Sunday for models and hip-hop night), but in my opinion it's over-rated and not a patch on PH-D Lounge upstairs, where younger, even hotter women dance to better DJs in a much bigger space, with the added bonus of a view. ⌂ *electricroomnyc.com; 212- 229-2511; 355 West 16th St..; till 4 AM.*

PH-D Lounge Rooftop, Dance Club, Models and Bottles

The rooftop of the Dream Hotel hosts one of the trendiest party spots in the city for the young and beautiful. At peak times, and/or if you're not with females, you'll be asked to rack up a bar tab of around $100 per head. It's also $20 for a drink, and because there's no dance floor, people just dance around tables and where there's space. That may sound awful, but surprisingly, it met my expectations. There's a ton of hotties in their early twenties, the music is decent, and the view and ambiance are great. Like most of these places, you can get in for free without hassle if you show up with a sexy female when the line is short. Would I go if I had to pay in? Hell no! I'd skip it and go to The Park. ⌂ *phdlounge.com; 212-229-2511; 355 W 16th St.; till 4 AM.*

The Jane ^{Dance Club}

A trendy party spot in a beautiful old-world hotel ballroom. The crowd is a little more mature than other clubs in the area, but it's a well-known hookup scene. Arrive before 11 p.m. if you want to avoid a massive line and get in. Like most Meatpacking places, it's not single men friendly, so try and roll with girls. You can also get in if you get there before 9 p.m. when the bouncers arrive. ⌂ *thejanenyc.com; 212-924-6700; 113 Jane St.; Thurs-Sat till 4 AM.*

Places Best Avoided

Don't have $1,500 for a table? Not on the list? Prefer to dance rather than sit? Keep moving pal! Here's a list of places you'll want to avoid unless you have money to burn, a connection, or roll with a model on your arm. I've only got in the door of some of these places because I knew a promoter. Don't waste your time with the following: *Catch Rooftop, Gilded Lady, Provocateur, The Boom Boom Room, Simyone Lounge, Avenue, 1 Oak, and Up & Down.*

East Village and the Lower East Side (LES)

"Meatpacking is Disneyland," as one buxom Cielo bartender put it. "This place for tourists and posers. *Real* New Yorkers go to the east side." For the most part I'd have to agree with her. Most revelers consider the east side 'authentic' New York. Nowhere in the city can you find a better variety of *quality* venues: most of which are tucked away and have a very in-the-know kind of feel.

Up until the 1960's, the whole area below 14th Street was considered the Lower East Side, but as uppity artsy types starting moving north of Houston Street, the term "East Village" was employed to distinguish the northern part from the slummy image of the Lower East Side (LES). Today, the two areas blend together when it comes to nightlife. LES—my favorite area to party in Manhattan—is a little edgier and tends to attract a slightly younger crowd, whereas East Village is more eclectic and spread out.

East Village is bounded by 14th Street to the north, Houston Street to the south, Greenwich to the west, and the East River to the east (although anything past Avenue C is a dead zone for nightlife). East Village is separated into two parts: East Village West (simply referred to as East Village) and Alphabet City, with the latter describing anything east of 1st Avenue; here, the main streets are broken down into Avenues A, B, C, and D (hence the name Alphabet City).

In East Village, most of the action centers around 3rd Avenue and Astor Place. This area has the most 'mainstream' party scene on the east side. For a big night out head to NYC's biggest nightclub **Webster Hall**. There's also lively parties at **the 13th Step** and the back room dance floors of **Bar None** and **Village Pourhouse**. To warm up, I highly recommend you check out Japanese speakeasy

Angel's Share and atmospheric **McSorley's Ale House** (the oldest pub in the city). If you want to catch a buzz, you can also get five shots of hard liquor for $10 at **Continental Bar**.

Moving east into Alphabet City, reserve a spot at secretive **PDT** to get the night off to a memorable start. If they put you on the waitlist, there's another speakeasy called **Blind Barber** around the corner. Other cools spots are **The Wayland** and **Double Down Saloon**. The downside of Alphabet City is that it's pretty quiet during the week.

Moving south of Houston Street, you enter the grimy underworld of the Lower East Side. This area can also be separated into two parts. The western area around Sara D. Roosevelt Park is technically Bowery (after the street), although most people refer to it as part of the LES due to the nightlife there. Technically, however, the actual Lower East Side is anything east of Allen Street.

In Bowery, good places to party are **bOb Bar**, **Sweet & Vicious**, and **Katra**. For a speakeasy vibe, check out **Attaboy**.

On the LES, the crowd gets younger, and the bars get cooler. There are almost too many recommendations. At some point, definitely check out NYC's coolest speakeasy **Back Room.** If you want to get drunk on the cheap, there's punk bar **Welcome to the Johnson's** and frat-fest **Down the Hatch.** If it's the weekend, and it's before 10 p.m., your next stop should be **Manhanta** Balkan bar. This is a good place to end up, but if you're not digging the vibe, head to club hook-up spots **The Delancey** or **Fat Baby.** During the week, **Pianos** consistently draws a dance crowd upstairs, making it my no.1 pick in the area.

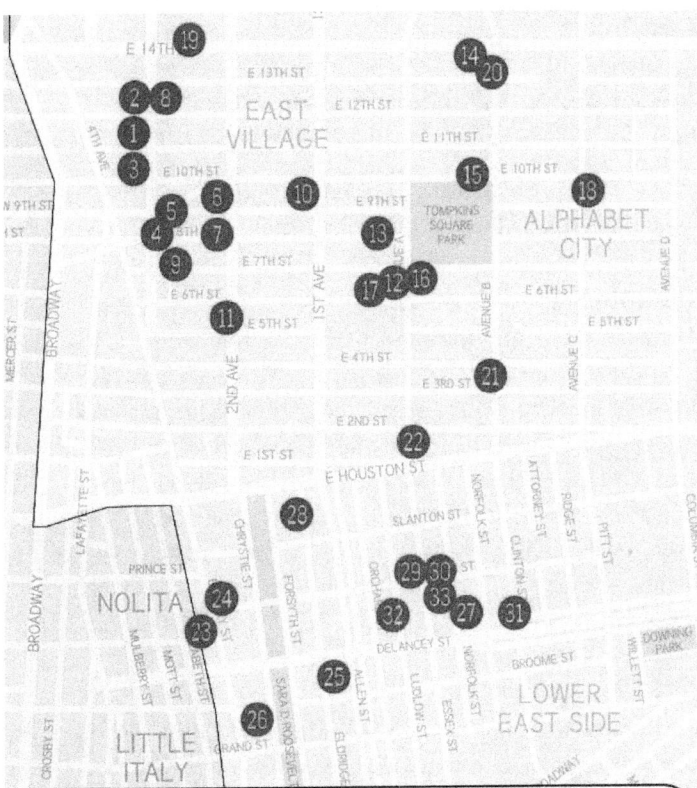

1. Webster Hall
2. Bar None
3. Pourhouse
4. Continental
5. Angel's Share
6. The 13th Step
7. Kyber Pass
8. Penny Farthing
9. McSorley's
10. Cayote Ugly
11. Lit Lounge
12. Pyramid Club
13. PDT
14. Otto's Shrunken Head
15. Blind Barber
16. Niagara
17. Death & Co.
18. The Wayland
19. Beauty Bar
20. Mona's
21. No Malice Palace
22. Double Down Saloon
23. Sweet & Vicious
24. Katra
25. Attaboy
26. Tropical 128
27. Back Room
28. bOb Bar
29. Fat Baby
30. Mehanata
31. The Delancey
32. Mehanata
33. Welcome to The Johnson's

Area Profile
Population: 102k
Average Age: 36, with 37% aged between 20 and 35.
Race: 39% White, 29% Hispanic, 22% Asian, 8% Black, 2% other.

East Village (West of 1st Ave)

The 13th Step College Bar, Dive Bar

The largest and most lively establishment from the NYC Best Bars group: the same crew behind Off the Wagon, Down the Hatch, Stumble Inn, etc. While I'm not the biggest fan of the backwards-cap clientele, this is one of the most consistently busy bars in the East Village. They also have good drink specials and there are lots of female students around. The ratio can be brutal and it gets overcrowded on weekends, but it's a great option on Tuesday nights when a crowd show up for $1 beers. ◌ *nycbestbar.com/13thstep; 212- 387-7300; 149 2ⁿᵈ Ave.; till 4 AM.*

McSorley's Ale House Dive Bar, TOP PICK!

The oldest Irish tavern in NYC. There's sawdust on the floor, communal tables, and only two beer choices: light or dark. It's no pick-up joint, but it's a mandatory stop-off on an East Village pub crawl. Just be warned that they close early at 1 a.m.. ◌ *212-473-9148; 15 E 7th St.; till 1 AM.*

Penny Farthing College Bar

Another consistently busy bar with people in their mid-to-late twenties. It's trendier than other bars in the area, so expect more high heels and better-looking women. When busy on weekend, it's probably the best place to pick up quality women on 3ʳᵈ Ave. (if it doesn't get overcrowded). ◌ *thepennyfarthingnyc.com; 212-228-8020; 103 3rd Avenue (Btwn 12ᵗʰ and 13ᵗʰ St.); till 4 AM.*

Webster Hall ^{Dance Club}

The biggest nightclub in New York City. It's four stories of bedlam, with DJs, live bands, and more young women than you can chat up in a year. The also admit girls over 18 and are lax about the dress code. I usually don't like mega-clubs, but I've had fun here. It's not nearly as pretentious or expensive as it's Meatpacking counterparts and Pacha (although still expect to pay $8 for a beer). Sometimes they have drink specials on the bottom floor. Beforehand, make sure you go to their website to get discounted admission. Visit websterhall.com/guestlist to get $5 tickets for Friday and Saturday (or pay up to $35 at the door like an idiot). *websterhall.com; 212-353-1600; 125 E 11th St; till 4 AM.*

Continental ^{Dive Bar}

This punk-rock dive is a shit-hole with little ambiance, but you can get five shots of hard liquor for $10, so you can't complain. This is the place to get loaded on the cheap in the area. Sunday to Thursday all drafts are only $2.50. ⌂ *continentalnyc.com; 212-529-6924; 25 3rd Ave. (Btwn St. Marks & 3rd Av); till 4 AM.*

Lit Lounge ^{Disco Bar}

A dingy little disco lounge that's buzzing Thursday to Sunday. It's a good place for hooking up (I had sex in the bathrooms), and there's a dance floor and a pool table. ⌂ *litloungenyc.com; 212-777-7987; 93 2nd Ave; till 4 AM.*

Coyote Ugly ^{Themed Bar, Dive Bar}

A filthy sleaze-pit with 6's dancing on the counter. It's a replica of the recently closed Hogs and Heifers but with fewer tourists. It's fun for a round or two if you're looking for something a little different. ⌂ *coyoteuglysaloon.com/newyork; 212-477-4431; 153 1st Ave. (Btwn 9th & 10th); till 4 AM.*

Village Pourhouse ^{College Bar, Dance Club}

This divey sports bar isn't up to much, but on the weekend there's a decent party in the back, with a DJ, dancing, and loads of young singles. ⌂ *villagepourhouse.com; 212-979-2337; 982 Amsterdam Ave.; Fri & Sat till 4 AM.*

Bar None ^{Dive Bar, Dance Club, TOP PICK!}

It's a little small, but there's cheap booze, a diverse crowd, and a dance floor in the back. My wingman Dom loves this spot for picking up (especially for black chicks). ⌂ *barnone-nyc.com; 212-777-6663; 5 93 3rd Ave. (Btwn 12th & 13th St.); till 4 AM.*

Alphabet City

PDT ^{Speakeasy, Date Spot, TOP PICK!}

PDT (an acronym for 'please don't tell') has the coolest entrance of any speakeasy in the city. Enter a hot dog place called Crif Dogs and you'll notice an old telephone booth in the corner. Pick up the phone, dial '1', and see what happens. Just be sure to ring ahead and make a reservation. It's a low-key spot, but worth the experience if you can get in. Anytime I have friends visiting the city I try to bring them here. ⌂ *pdtnyc.com; 212-614-0386; 113 St Marks Pl.; Mon-Fri till 2 AM, Sat & Sun till 4 AM.*

Blind Barber ^{Speakeasy, Dance Club}

This place is a hybrid of a prohibition-style speakeasy and a small dance club. Expect a yuppie crowd dancing to old school hip-hop. The entrance is through the back of a barber shop, but the security guard in the front of the building gives the game away. Nonetheless, the concept is pretty cool and it's a great alternative if you can't get into PDT or are more interested in picking up. ⌂ *blindbarber.com; 212-228-2123; 339 E 10th St.; till 4 AM.*

Death & Co. Cocktail Bar, Rock Bar, Date Spot

This gothic-style cocktail lounge claims to be a speakeasy, but the doors are clearly marked, and the security guard and people smoking out front make it blatantly visible. While I'm fan of the décor, the hard rock playlist, and the young female clientele, I feel this place is overrated. There's often a wait-list to get in, the table stools are uncomfortable, and at $15 a cocktail, you'd be better off going to a genuine speakeasy like nearby PDT or Angel's Share instead (in my experience they have better drinks, too). All that said, if there's no wait and you can get a seat at the bar, it's worth a visit for a beer. ⌂ *deathandcompany.com; 212-388-0882; 433 E 6th St.; Sun-Thurs till 1 AM, Fri & Sat till 2 AM.*

Double Down Saloon Dive Bar, Rock Bar

A hardcore punk rock bar with graffiti on the walls, light BDSM porn on the TVs, and 'ass juice' shots. There's also a pool table. It attracts an alternative crowd, but it's pretty quiet outside the weekend. ⌂ *doubledownsaloon.com; 212-982-0543; 14 Avenue A; till 4 AM.*

Otto's Shrunken Head Themed Bar, Dive Bar, Live Music

One of the NYC's oddest establishments. Imagine a tiki bar run by goths living in the 1980's. The crowd is very alternative and the vibes vary massively depending on the night. Look online to see what parties are going on. ⌂ *ottosshrunkenhead.com; 212-228-2240; 538 E 14th St.; till 4 AM.*

Mona's Dive Bar, Live Music

An old school dive with drink specials, live music, and a pool table. Monday is bluegrass night and one of the best sessions in the city. Tuesday is jazz night. Times vary—and the crowd leaves with the band—so check the Facebook page for times. ⌂ *Facebook: Mona's Bar NYC; 212-353-3780; 224 Avenue B (Btwn 13th and 14th); till 4 AM.*

Beauty Bar Dive Bar, Dance Club

A bizarre hybrid of a beauty salon and a dive bar. They offer a manicure and a cocktail for $10, so women love it. However, the real draw here is the back room dance floor on weekends. ⌂ *thebeautybar.com; 212-539-1389; 231 E 14th St; till 4 AM.*

The Wayland Bar, Cocktail Bar, Live Music, TOP PICK!

The most loved neighborhood bar in Alphabet City and one of the few places that live up to the hype. Aside from its rustic southern charm, there's live music Sunday to Wednesday, and their craft cocktails beat out many speakeasies (try the garden variety margarita). There's also $5 PBR tall-boys for those on a budget. On weekends it's packed, but midweek it's a lot more chill, and the place dies a death when the band finishes at 1 a.m. I'd recommend it as a place to visit mid pub crawl. ⌂ *thewaylandnyc.com; 212-777-7022; 700 E 9th St. (Av. C); till 4 AM.*

No Malice Palace Disco Bar

A divvy dance club with a laid-back vibe and a diverse crowd dancing to old-school hip-hop, dancehall, and reggaeton. Drinks are inexpensive, but there's a $5 cover on weekends. ⌂ *nomalice.com; 212-254-9184; 197 E 3rd St (Btwn Ave. A and Ave. B); Sun-Thurs till 3 AM, Fri & Sat till 4 AM.*

Niagara Dive Bar, Dance Club

On weeknights, this place is pretty laid-back, but on weekends the dance floor is the back is hoping. ⌂ *niagaranyc.com; 212-420-9517; 112 Avenue A; till 4 AM.*

Pyramid Club Themed Bar, Dance Club

An unpretentious 80's dance club with reasonably priced drinks. It's a bit corny, and the crowd is so-so, but fun all the same. ⌂ *thepyramidclub.com; 212-228-4888; 101 Avenue A (Btwn 6th and 7th St.); till 4 AM.*

Bowery

Home Sweet Home ^{Dive Bar}

An underground hipster hangout with taxidermy on the walls and people in their late twenties dancing to oldies. It's a popular spot, but it's certainly not worth the cover charge on weekends. ⌂ *homesweethomebar.com; 131 Chrystie St.; till 4 AM.*

Katra ^{Lounge, Dance Club}

A long and narrow Moroccan-themed dance lounge with two floors. The music is mainly hip-hop, with some reggaeton and Soca thrown in. Tuesday is *Kompa* night and attracts a lot of Haitians. It's overpriced and they sometimes charge admission, but it's the best place in the area if you have a hunger for some dark chocolate. ⌂ *katranyc.com; 212-473-3113; 217 Bowery Street; till 4 AM, closed Sun & Mon.*

Attaboy ^{Speakeasy}

A tiny speakeasy hid on a quiet street behind a nondescript door. It's not touristy or gimmicky like its rivals, and rather than offering you a menu the bartenders will make custom cocktails based on what flavors you like. It fills up fast on weekends, so go on an off-night. ⌂ *134 Eldridge St.; till 3.30 AM.*

bOb Bar ^{Dance Club}

A tiny dance club with a lax door policy, great DJs, and a diverse crowd. People either love or hate this crowded little sweat-box. The music is R&B/hip-hop focused with a dash of reggae. There's a $5 cover on weekends and drinks ain't cheap, but it's a great option for a Wednesday or Thursday if you're already drunk and ready to move. When this place is full, the spillover ends up in its sister bar **247 Lounge**, which has the exact same crowd, music, and set-up. ⌂ *bobbarnyc.com; 212-529-1807; 235 Eldridge St; Thurs-Sat till 4 AM.*

Tropical 128 ^{Lounge, Themed Bar, Dance Club}

A cave bar with palm trees and water features. It can be hit or miss, but it's reasonable, there's no cover, and it has a sizable dance floor that attracts all types. It's worth checking out if you happen to be nearby. △ *tropical128nyc.com; 212-925-8219; 128 Elizabeth St.; Sun-Thurs till 2 AM, Fri & Sat till 4 AM.*

Sweet & Vicious ^{Disco Bar}

A small LES bar that's popular for dancing and letting loose. It has a mixed crowd and some nice girls, and the layout conducive for picking up. It's worth a visit. △ *sweetandviciousnyc.com; 212-334-7915; 5 Spring St.; till 4 AM.*

Lower East Side

Welcome to the Johnson's ^{Dive Bar}

The quintessential LES dive bar: a grimy den that looks like it was converted from a punk rocker's basement. There's a kitchen fridge for beers, a pool table, torn sofas, and the crowd looks like the cast from Rocky Horror Picture Show. It's not a pick up spot, but a can of PBR is only $2. △ *212-420-9911; 123 Rivington St.; till 4 AM.*

Back Room ^{Speakeasy, TOP PICK!}

The least pretentious—and arguably coolest—speakeasy in the city. It's also one of only two NYC speakeasies still in existence that operated during prohibition. Look for a small sign marked 'Lower East Side Toy Company' with stairs leading down to a grubby underground alleyway. Go past the garbage cans and up another stairs to find the front door. You'll enter a large dimly-lit room with 20-somethings sipping booze from teacups and coffee mugs. There's live jazz on Mondays and DJs on the weekend. During winter the place is jammed. △ *backroomnyc.com; 212-228-5098; 102 Norfolk St; (Btwn Delancey and Rivington St.); Sun-Wed till 2 AM, Thurs till 3 AM, Fri & Sat till 4 AM.*

Hair of the Dog Dive Bar, College Bar

The LES installment from the NYC Best Bar group. It's a good place to pregame during the week because of the drink specials, but on weekends it's a shit-show: crammed like sardines with college kids grinding to chart music. It's a serious hook-up spot, but don't expect to find any beauty queens. ⌂ *nycbestbar.com/hairofthedog; 212-477-7771; 168 Orchard St; till 4 AM.*

Mehanata Themed Bar, Dance Club

A unique Bulgarian-gypsy disco bar with a ski-cabin vibe and a Eurocentric crowd. The ground level has swings for seats at the bar, a small dance floor, and live music followed by DJs that play everything from Balkan beats to Bachata. Downstairs, things are a lot messier, with chart music, stripper poles, and people stumbling on the dance floor. The culprit for this inebriation is the infamous 'ice cage': a sub-zero room lined with vodka bottles, where for $20 bartenders give you a military outfit and let you do unlimited shots for two minutes. It's definitely zany and a place you should check out, but try to get here before 10 p.m. when they start charging at the door. ⌂ *mehanata.com; 212-625-0981; 113 Ludlow St.; Thurs-Sat till 4 AM.*

Pianos Live Music, Dance Club, TOP PICK!

Ahh, reliable Pianos: the poster child of LES. This hipster hangout is a LES favorite for good reason. I love this place because it's inexpensive, there's no cover, and most importantly, it draws a lively crowd every single night. There's also three different rooms with three different types of music. Upstairs is my favorite area. Be warned that on weekends the line to get in is ridiculous. ⌂ *pianosnyc.com.com; 212-505-3733; 158 Ludlow St; till 4 AM.*

Fat Baby Dance Club, Live Music

A lively little dance spot with two floors, a top 40s playlist, and no cover. I'd recommend hitting this place later in the night when you're already buzzed. It can get a little crowded, but it attracts a lot of women wanting to party. I came here my first month in NYC, and within twenty minutes I met a Colombian and banged her in the bathroom. Argh! ⌂ *fatbabynyc.com; 212-533-1888; 112 Rivington St.; Thurs-Sat till 4 AM.*

The Delancey Dance Club, TOP PICK!

A narrow rough-and-ready tri-level dance club that's refreshingly laid-back. The crowd is pretty diverse. Go downstairs for hip-hop and live music, hit ground level for chart and cheese, or head upstairs to find a relaxed rooftop garden lounge with Moroccan-style décor (a great place to bring a girl you've pulled from below). Admission is free, and the crowd is prettier than average. There are a few negatives: there's no draft beer, sometimes they charge to go upstairs, and the mid-level dance floor can get uncomfortably packed. Aside for those issues, I still highly recommend it if you want something high-energy in the area. ⌂ *thedelancey.com; 212-254-9920; 168 Delancey St; Thurs-Sat till 4 AM.*

Chelsea and Midtown West

Greenwich Village was traditionally the gay capital of NYC, but the rainbow banners have spread well north of 14th Street. Chelsea is now the main 'gayborhood' of Manhattan, and it's top, Hell's kitchen (or 'Hellsea' with a lisp), has become just as limp-wristed. That said, the area still hosts some of the city's most popular venues, and there're a few great bars to pick up in. This chapter also includes Times Square and anything west of 6th Ave.

Chelsea constitutes the area from 14th street to 34th street, but for the nightlife purposes, I've excluded southwest Chelsea because the club scene there is more Meatpacking than Chelsea (see the Greenwich Village chapter for info). As for the rest of Chelsea, if you like vagina, good venues are few and far between. Aside from mega clubs like **Marquee** and **Slake**, there aren't many reasons for you to be here at night. If you do find yourself stuck here, you can grab a pint at themed bar **Trailer Park Lounge** or **World of Beer**.

North of 34th Street, things are a lot more lively. Most of the action happens around the restaurant strip of 9th Avenue. For a good pub crawl, start the night at **Rudy's** for a few $5 beer and shot combos and a free hot dog. If it's the weekend, move on and warm up with a few approaches at surf bar **Reunion** or **Mercury Lounge** (the former for lighter skin, the latter for darker). From 9th Ave., take a final pit-spot in one of the many bars on **Restaurant Row**, before ending the night in the always unmemorable **Mean Fiddler**.

If you're looking to ramp things up a notch and have a bit more to spend, head farther west. Start your night with some brews and bowling at **Lucky Strike** on 12th. From there, get some cheeky cheapies in at **McQuaid's Pub** before heading to **Press Lounge rooftop** to take in the scenery. End the night at mega-clubs **Pacha** or **Stage 48** (just don't go sober and get tickets online beforehand).

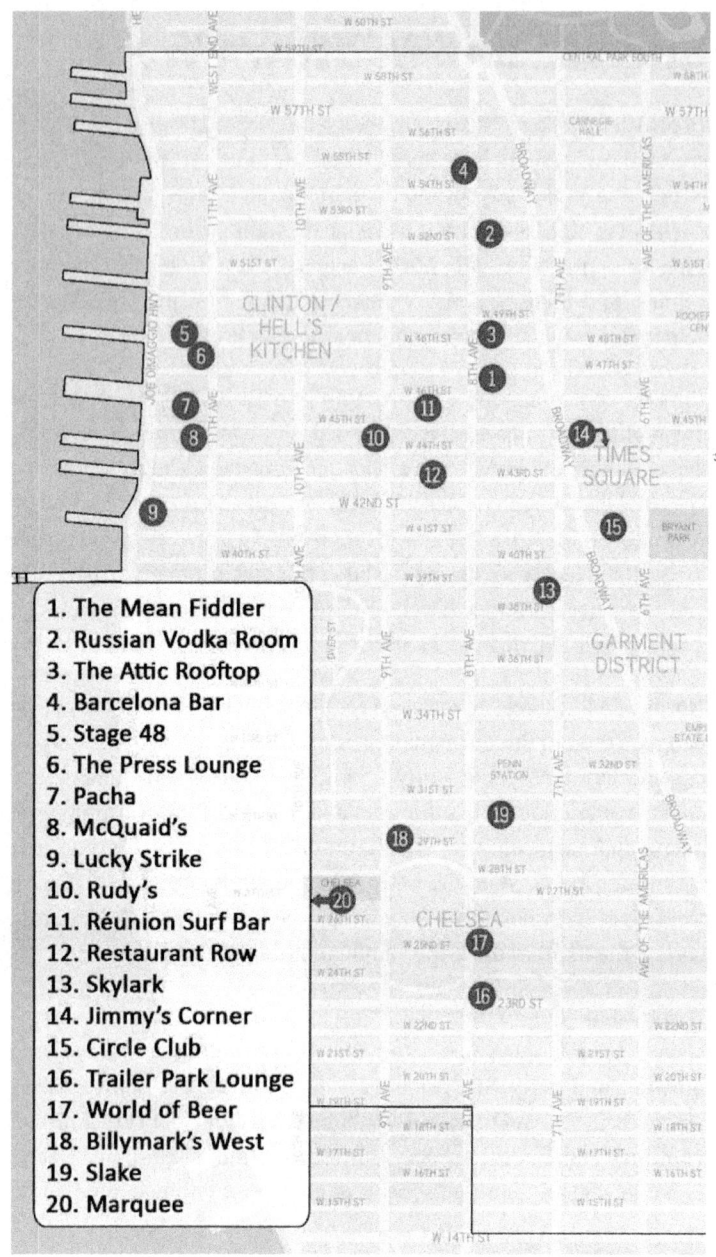

1. The Mean Fiddler
2. Russian Vodka Room
3. The Attic Rooftop
4. Barcelona Bar
5. Stage 48
6. The Press Lounge
7. Pacha
8. McQuaid's
9. Lucky Strike
10. Rudy's
11. Réunion Surf Bar
12. Restaurant Row
13. Skylark
14. Jimmy's Corner
15. Circle Club
16. Trailer Park Lounge
17. World of Beer
18. Billymark's West
19. Slake
20. Marquee

Area Profile
Population: 144k
Average Age: 37, with 36% aged between 20 and 35.
Race: 64% White, 15% Hispanic, 13% Asian, 5% Black, 3% other.

Hell's Kitchen

Rudy's ^{Dive Bar, TOP PICK!}

The go-to dive bar in the area. You can get a pint and a shot for just $5, pitchers from $8, and there's free hot dogs. Pink Floyd is always playing, too. (What more could you want?) It's also consistently busy and attracts an extremely diverse crowd: from aging bikers to Brazilian and European students on a budget. You'll find a few cuties about, too. It's a great place to both start and end your night. ⌂ *rudysbarnyc.com; 646-707-0890; 627 9th Av. (btw 44th & 45t); till 4 AM.*

Réunion Surf Bar ^{Themed Bar}

An underground surfer themed bar designed to look like a beach shack. It's a little bit corny and feels more Hawaiian than Creole, but it's something different for NYC, and the crowd is noticeably younger and more attractive than the one in Rudy's across the street. It's reasonably busy on the weekend, but midweek the crowd disbands before midnight. ⌂ *reunionbar.com; 212-582-3200; 357 W 44th St.; till 2 AM Sun-Wed, 4 AM Thurs-Sat.*

The Press Lounge ^{Rooftop, Lounge}

Right beside Stage 48 is The Press Lounge. It's your typical rooftop vibe, with great views you pay $11 a beer for. There's a lot of well-dressed young professionals, but it's by no means a late night party spot. There are better rooftops, but if you're in the area it's a good place for a view. ⌂ *thepresslounge.com; 212-757-2224; 653 11ᵗʰ Ave.; till 12-3 AM depending on the day.*

Restaurant Row ^{Bar Strip}

A bar and restaurant strip on W 46th Street between 8th and 9th Avenue. It's good for a stop-off on your way to or from Hell's Kitchen to the subway. New Orleans inspired **Bourbon Street** is the biggest spot, offering cheap drinks and attracting the most singles. For something a little classier, check out **Swing 46**. My favorite spot to grab a pint is **House of Brews** ($5 for all drafts after midnight). ⌂ *restaurantrownyc.com; W 46th St, between 8th and 9th Aves.; till 4 AM.*

Pacha ^{Dance Club}

One of the only places open after 4 a.m. This enormous multilevel club is modeled after the Ibiza rave mecca and is almost as big as Webster Hall. There're big name DJs, airport-level security check-ins, exorbitant drink prices, and a very energetic young crowd. Pregame heavily and go to their website to get cheap (or free) tickets. Otherwise, you'll be paying $40 at the door and $10 for a Bud Light. Despite my skepticism about this place I admittedly had a good time here, but I wouldn't recommend it going unless you're revved up on caffeine, booze, and/or MDMA. ⌂ *pachanyc.com; 212-209-7500; 618 618 W 46th St.(Btwn West St. and 11th Ave.); Thurs-Sat till 6-8 AM.*

Stage 48 ^{Dance Club}

A slightly more laid-back alternative to Pacha around the corner, this so-called 'concert venue' is really more of a big club. The crowd completely changes depending on the event and who is playing as they host everything from gay nights to heavy metal bands. The night I went, there was a reggae party and felt like I was back in Kingston. Go online for more info and to get discounted admission. ⌂ *stage48.com; 212-957-1800; 605 West 48th St. (Btwn West St. and 11th Ave.).; till ?.*

McQuaid's Public House Dive Bar

Wanna get drunk before hitting Pacha or Stage 48? This grubby little Irish pub is your best (and only) option. Everything on the menu is only $5, from Grey Goose to Bud Light. Be aware that it closes at midnight. ⌂ *212-582-6359; 589 11th Ave.; till 12 AM.*

Skylark Rooftop, Cocktail Lounge, Date Spot

A decent rooftop option near Times Square with a great view of the Empire State Building. The drinks are pricey, but the panorama is amazing. It's a good date spot. ⌂ *theskylarknyc.com; 212-257-4577; 200 W 39th St.; Mon & Tues till 12 AM, Wed-Fri till 1 AM.*

Booze Cruises

There are several companies offering booze cruises in summer. Check online to see what's going on.

Times Square & Around

The Mean Fiddler Disco Bar, Irish Pub, TOP PICK!

Ah, the Fiddler. Leave your memory and inhibitions at the door. This place is a major party spot for Irish expats, tourists, and New Yorkers looking for a place to get completely shit-faced and hookup without being judged for it. It's the kind of place you could fall off your chair and they'll still keep pouring your drinks. The small dance floor it also one of the few places you can find a pulse midweek. It's a great place to end your night, but the only downside is that drinks are Times Square prices. ⌂ *themeanfiddlernyc.com; 212-354-2950; 266 W 47th St; till 4 AM.*

Jimmy's Corner Bar Dive Bar

This boxing themed dive bar is one of the only places for cheap drinks around Times Square. It's not too touristy either. ⌂ *facebook.com/jimmyscornernyc; 212-221-9510; 140 W 44th St; till 4 AM.*

The Attic Rooftop _{Bar Rooftop, Dance Club}

A world away from the Mean Fiddler nearby, the Attic is a pretentious rooftop club with prices and attitudes that match the altitude. There's a lot of bottle service, showing off, and a $20 cover for guys, but it's not as snobby as Meatpacking, and it has the sexiest women in the area (there's a 'no flats' policy). The DJs are pretty solid, too. Drag a couple of girls with you to get in the door. ⌂ *theattic-nyc.com; 212-956-1300; 251 W 48th St; Thurs-Sat till 4 AM.*

Russian Vodka Room _{Themed Bar, Lounge, Date Spot}

Something a little different. This dark, intimate little spot has live piano music, cold platters, and an extensive list of bizarre flavored vodkas (horseradish and caramelized walnuts, anyone?). It's a cool place for a date or an interesting place to pregame. ⌂ *russianvodkaroom.com; 212-307-5835; 265 W 52nd St.; Mon-Thurs till 2 AM, Fri-Sun till 4 AM.*

Barcelona Bar _{Dive Bar, Themed Bar}

Aside from the Russian Vodka Room, this is the only other place worth mentioning north of Times Square. It's tiny, packed, and not near anything, but it's a memorable place if you order the Harry Potter or Two Towers shots (expect lots of fire). Don't go out of your way to come here, however. ⌂ *barcelonabarnyc.com; 212-245-3212; 5 Spring St.; till 4 AM*

Circle Club _{Dance Club}

The no.1 spot for Korean girls. There's a big dance floor and plenty of high heels, but there's a $20 cover and drinks are pricey. ⌂ *thecirclenyc.com; 212-575-4779; 135 W 41st St.; Thurs-Sat till 4.30 AM.*

Chelsea

Trailer Park Lounge ^{Themed Bar, Dive Bar}

This kitschy dive bar has a 1950's trailer park theme. It's not a bad option if you're stuck in Chelsea. There isn't much aside from cheap beer and a unique vibe, but you won't find much else around. ⌂ *trailerparklounge.com; 212-463-8000; 271 W 23rd St.; till 2 AM.*

World of Beer ^{Themed Bar}

This place only opened in late 2015 and is a welcome oasis in the vaginal wasteland of Chelsea. With 550+ beers available, no place in the city has a better selection. ⌂ *worldofbeer.com; 212-255-2337; 316 8th Av. (Btwn 25th and 26th St.); till ?.*

Billymark's West ^{Dive Bar}

A serious dive that's good for cheap drinks if you're around Penn Station or pregaming before hitting one of the nearby clubs. ⌂ *212-629-0118; 332 9th Ave. (Btwn 29th and 30th); till 4 AM.*

Marquee ^{Dance Club}

A mega-club modeled after the one in Las Vegas that only gets a mention because of its notoriety. It's like Pacha with more tables and only one DJ. Expect to pay a $60 cover and $9 for bottled water (tickets online for $20-30). It's only worth going to if you're fucked up on molly on a Wednesday. ⌂ *marqueeny.com; 646-473-0202; 289 10th Ave. (Btwn 26th and 27th); Wed-Sat 4 AM.*

Slake ^{Dance Club}

A smaller, toned-down version of nearby Marquee with multiple floors. It's owned by the same people behind Webster Hall. Tickets are available online for $15-20. ⌂ *slakenyc.com; 212-695-8970; 251 W 30th St.; Thurs-Sat till 4 AM.*

Midtown East and Southeast

North of East Village decent nightlife options are limited. There's a bit of action near the center of the island along the arteries of 5th and 6th Ave., and on 3rd Ave in the east, but to be honest, I would advise you to avoid this part of town if you're only here for a short period. There are so many better parts of the city for nightlife. That said, if you find yourself stuck in this part of town I've included a few places worth checking out.

Below 42nd Street is a confusing cluster-fuck of overlapping neighborhoods usually referred to as the Gramercy/Murray Hill area, but I've termed it 'Midtown Southeast' to make it simple and more succinct. From 14th to 23rd Street are the areas of Flatiron, Gramercy, and Union Square. Aside from a bit of overflow from East Village on 14th Street, there's nothing here worth going to. The only exception is speakeasy **Raine's Law Room**. From 23rd to 42nd Street, there are the largely residential neighborhoods of Kips Bay and Murray Hill to the east, and to the west, near the center of the island, there are the areas of NoMad (North of Madison square garden), Koreatown, and south of Bryant Park. Most of the action in this part of town takes place along **3rd Avenue**. Here the best option is hookup joint **Tonic East**. For the best view in town, head to rooftop lounge **230 Fifth**.

Above 42nd Street lies the commercial and retail heart of the city. Here you'll find the likes of Grand Central and the Rockefeller Center. In terms of nightlife, **Johnny Utah's** and **Turtle Bay Tavern** are the most popular venues for cheap drinks and college party vibes. The latter is a good choice almost any night of the week and attracts a lot of horny bridge and tunnel girls. For high heels and the best-looking women, there's pretentious **Lavo**.

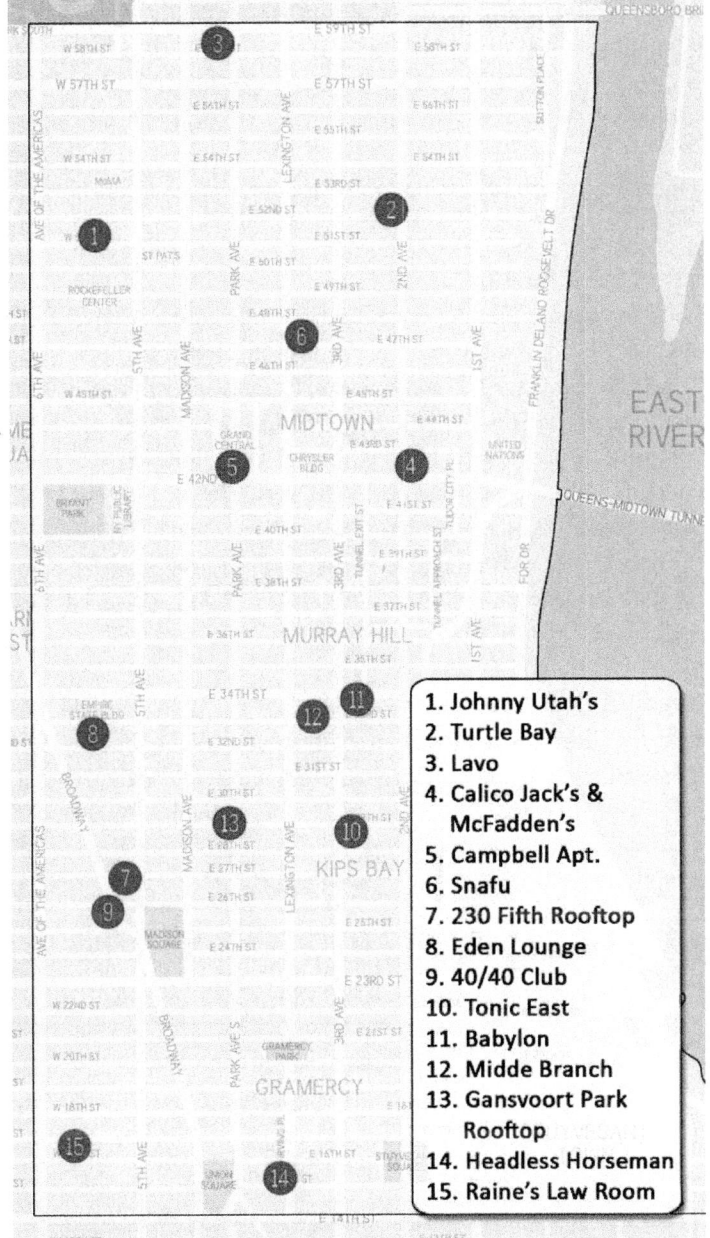

1. Johnny Utah's
2. Turtle Bay
3. Lavo
4. Calico Jack's &
   McFadden's
5. Campbell Apt.
6. Snafu
7. 230 Fifth Rooftop
8. Eden Lounge
9. 40/40 Club
10. Tonic East
11. Babylon
12. Midde Branch
13. Gansvoort Park
    Rooftop
14. Headless Horseman
15. Raine's Law Room

Area Profile

Population: 146k.

Average Age: 36, with 36% aged between 20 and 35.

Race: 64% White, 15% Hispanic, 13% Asian, 5% Black, 3% other.

Midtown Southeast (14th to 42nd Street)

Raine's Law Room Speakeasy, Date Spot

Look for a stairs leading down to an unmarked black door. Ring the doorbell. A few seconds later you'll be greeted by the host. If there's no space, they'll take your number and text you back within the hour. (There's a bar called **Rye House** down the street while you wait). When you get through the door, you'll be led to a sultry underground speakeasy that oozes old world charm. It's not a place to go alone, but it's perfect for an intimate cocktail with a date. While you're there, take a closer look at the wallpaper. ⌂ *raineslawroom.com; 48 W 17th St.; Sun till 1 AM, Mon-Wed till 2 AM, Thurs-Sat till 3 AM.*

Headless Horseman Themed Bar

If you're looking to go for a pint around Union Square, this medieval themed place is probably the most interesting option. Otherwise, I suggest you head to the bars around Astor Place in East Village. ⌂ *headlesshorsemannyc.com; 212-777-5101; 119 E 15th St.; Mon-Wed till 2 AM, Thurs-Sun till 4 AM.*

230 Fifth Rooftop Bar Rooftop, Lounge, Date Spot, TOP PICK!

It's not a party rooftop, but it's perched right across from the Empire State Building and is my favorite place for a skyline view when I've friends visiting. A pint will set you back $9, which is cheaper than most rooftops. ⌂ *230-fifth.com; 212-725-4300; 230 5th Ave. (Btwn 26th & 27th); till 4 AM.*

Middle Branch ^{Cocktail Bar, Date Spot}

This bar is from the same people behind Little Branch in West Village. It's not quite as good, but cocktails are reasonable at $12. ⌂ *212-213-1350; 154 E 33rd St.; till 2 AM.*

40/40 Club ^{Lounge}

I feel the need to mention this place only because it's famously owned by Jay Z and quite well known. There's tiered seating, overpriced drinks, and no dance floor. Thumbs down from me. In reality, it's more of a giant upscale sports bar than a nightclub, and only worth checking out after midnight on the weekend. ⌂ *the4040club.com; 917-618-6340; 6 W 25th St (cnr of Broadway); Fri & Sat till 4 AM.*

Eden Lounge ^{Dance Club}

If you like the sound of easy Korean girls, this is where all the Circle Club rejects end up. The sex ratio is poor. Pay the $20 cover at your peril. ⌂ *edenlounge-nyc.com; 212-290-1624; 28 W 33rd St; Thurs-Sat till 4 AM.*

Tonic East ^{Lounge, Disco Bar, Rooftop}

A more tolerable version of the Times Square franchise. It's known as the local hook-up joint for those in their 20's. On the second floor, there's a dance floor and above that there's a roof deck bar. It's probably the best bet in the area if you want to get laid. ⌂ *toniceast.com; 212-683-7090; 411 3rd Ave. (cnr of 29th); till 4 AM.*

Babylon ^{Hookah Lounge, Dance Club}

Like most hookah lounges, this place is hip-hop centric and attracts a good-looking non-white crowd. It's like Le Souk with a bigger dance floor. They also hire some very sexy 'belly dancers'. Sadly, there's usually a $20 cover for men on weekends. ⌂ *babylonhookahny.com; 212-933-0912; 208 E 34th St.; till 4 AM.*

Gansevoort Park Rooftop Dance Club, Rooftop

Meatpacking in Kips Bay: all tables, no dance floor, with a strict door and super-expensive drinks. I only came here because I was with a promoter. The girls are gorgeous, but the room is small, so people tend to stick by their tables and there's minimal interaction between strangers. Aside from the shitty club, it's good for the view during the day. ⌂ *gansevoorthotelgroup.com; 212-317-2900; 420 Park Ave. S.; till 4 AM.*

Midtown East (Above 42nd Street)

Johnny Utah's Themed Bar, College Bar

A large rodeo style bar with a mechanical bull, drink specials, and lots of plaid shirts. I'm not sure it's worth the $10 cover on weekends, but Thursdays there're dollar beers and plenty of drunk white college chicks from out of town. ⌂ *johnnyutahs.com; 212-265-8824; 25 W 51st (Btwn 5th & 6th Ave.); Mon-Thurs till 3 AM, Fri & Sat till 4 AM.*

Snafu Dive Bar

A narrow multilevel dive bar with video games and a pool table. It's a good alternative to bedlam of Turtle Bay around the corner. ⌂ *snafubarnyc.com; 212-317-9100; 127 E 47th St.(Btwn 3rd Ave. and Lex); till 4 AM.*

The Campbell Apartment Date Spot, Lounge

A swanky 1920's bar hidden inside Grand Central Station. Everybody is suited up and the booze ain't cheap, but I love the opulent nostalgic feel here. It's the kind of place where you imagine diplomats meet to drink aged scotch. If you're ever in Grand Central—and wearing appropriate attire—it's worth a pint to take in the ambiance. ⌂ *hospitalityholdings.com; 212-953-0409; Grand Central Terminal; Sun till 11 PM, Mon-Thurs till 1 AM, Fri & Sat till 2 AM.*

Calico Jack's & McFadden's Dive Bar, College Bar

If you want to get wasted for peanuts, and pick up near Grand Central, these two dives are your best options. Calico Jack's has $1 beers on Tuesdays and both offer 'pregame parties' with an open bar on Saturdays from only $10-15. ⌂ *calicojacksnyc.com / mcfaddens42.com; 800 2nd Ave. (corn of 42nd); till 4 AM.*

Turtle Bay Tavern Dive Bar, College Bar, Dance Club, TOP PICK!

On their website, Turtle Bay claims to be "the number one party bar in NYC". It's anything but classy, but if you're looking for a solid bet for a party, Turtle Bay provides. This bi-level meat market has drink deals, DJs, and busloads of horny bridge and tunnel college kids. A lot of girls are from Jersey and Staten Island and looking for a bed in Manhattan. Aside from Sunday and Monday, it's busy most nights, and while the girls are nothing to write home about, it's a great place to get laid. Tuesdays and Wednesdays there're dirt cheap beers, and on Thursdays there's an open bar for $20 before 1 a.m. ⌂ *turtlebaynyc.com; 212-223-4224; 987 2nd Ave. (Btwn 52nd and 53rd); till 4 AM.*

Lavo Dance Club, Models and Bottles

Owned by the Tao group, this elitist club is modeled after the one in Vegas. The crowd is mid-20s to late-30s, rich, and good-looking, and unlike its Meatpacking counterparts this place has a decent dance floor. There's a cover for general admission which varies between $20-50. If you're a group of guys, there's also a high likelihood you'll be asked to drop a bomb for a table. (It's also been reported that you can gain free entry if you eat at the restaurant upstairs.) ⌂ *lavony.com; 212-750-5588; 39 E 58th St; Thurs-Sat till 4 AM.*

Upper West Side (UWS)

Twenty years ago the Upper West Side was a trendy place to go out, but over time the population has gotten older, and the neighborhood has become more family-orientated. You would think having a major university would inject a bit of life into this part of town, but you'd be sadly mistaken. Not only is the bar scene remarkably underwhelming, but since the closure of Club C72 in 2014, the UWS is now officially dance floor free (and with new zoning laws regarding Cabaret licenses this won't be changing anytime soon).

Unless you end up staying here for a cheaper room rate, there's no good reason to be in this part of town at night when there are so many better options available. I know this area intimately, and it sucks. For those stuck up here, I recommend you check out the scene in Central Harlem instead, but if you're adamant to stay west of Central Park, I have provided you with the best options.

Below 96th Street, most of the action happens on Amsterdam Avenue around the early 80s. The main college hangout here is **Jake's Dilemma**, which has dollar beers on Monday nights. For a slightly more mature crowd, there's **E's Bar** up the road. If you want high heels and dancing, the sole option is the **Empire Hotel Rooftop** near Lincoln Center.

Above 96th Street, most of nightlife is just south of Columbia University and centered around the corner of Amsterdam Avenue and 110th Street. Depending on what night of the week it is, the most popular spots are **1020** (the unofficial campus bar), **Bernheim & Schwartz** (only on Wednesdays), and **Lion's Head**. I also have to mention my second home **The 'dam**, which is great for late night happy hour. If you're not digging the scene around here, there are better options on nearby Fredrick Douglas Street (see the Central Harlem section).

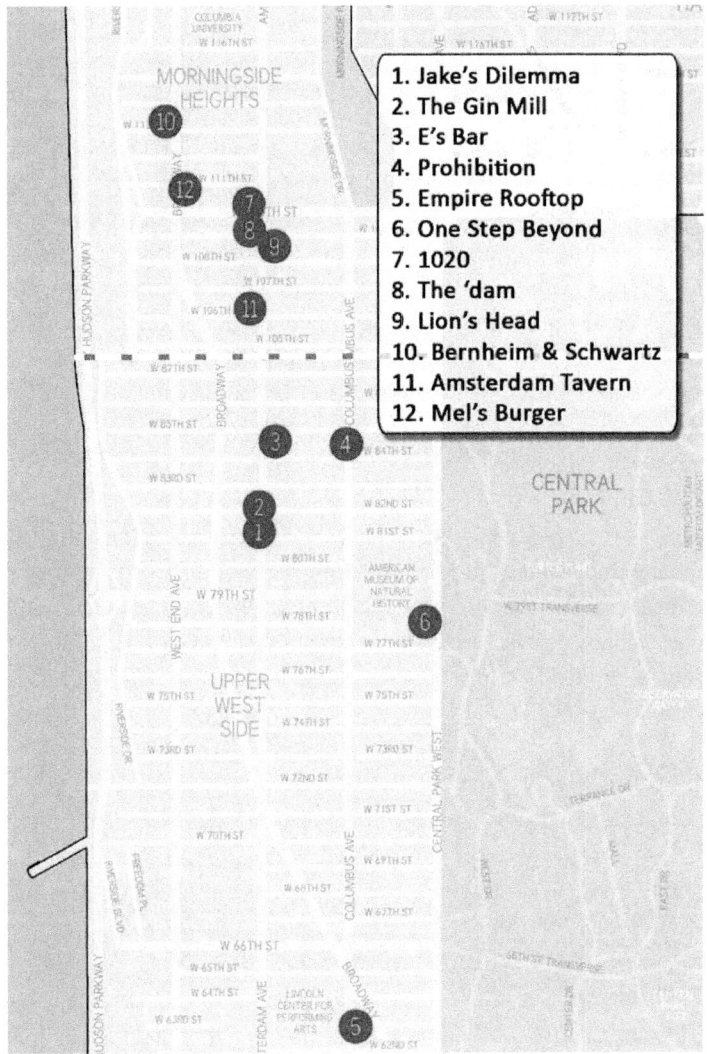

1. Jake's Dilemma
2. The Gin Mill
3. E's Bar
4. Prohibition
5. Empire Rooftop
6. One Step Beyond
7. 1020
8. The 'dam
9. Lion's Head
10. Bernheim & Schwartz
11. Amsterdam Tavern
12. Mel's Burger

Area Profile

Population: 191k
Average Age: 41, with 24% aged between 20 and 35.
Race: 69% White, 13% Hispanic, 9% Asian, 7% Black, 2% other.

Below 96th

Jake's Dilemma <small>College Bar, Dive Bar</small>

Jake's is probably the UWS's best college bar. It's owned by the NYC Best Bar group: the same crew behind Off the Wagon and The 13th Step. Expect the usual fare of beer pong, hot wings, and drink specials. I've always had fun in this place, but it can be very hit or miss with the crowd, and the sex ratio is usually abysmal. It's a great option for a Monday night when it's busy for dollar beer night, but go early. On weekends it's jammed. ⌂ *nycbestbar.com/jakes; 212-580-0556; 430 Amsterdam Ave.; till 4 AM.*

The Gin Mill <small>College Bar, Dive Bar</small>

Jake's little brother is just one block away. It's a lot smaller, quieter, and more restaurant-orientated, but on Thursdays for college night the front section fills up with students and occasionally tourists from the nearby hostel. Stick your head in if Jake's is dead. ⌂ *nycbestbar.com/ginmill; 212-580-9080; 442 Amsterdam Ave.; till 4 AM.*

E's Bar <small>Pub</small>

A good alternative to the typical college and wine bar scene on the UWS. It's nothing special, but there's drink deals, board games, and a rock 'n' roll vibe. ⌂ *e-barnyc.com; 212-877-0961; 511 Amsterdam Ave.; Sun-Wed till 12 AM, Thurs-Sat till 4 AM.*

Prohibition <small>Live Music</small>

This bar has live music most nights and is another great alternative to the frat bars in the area. It's a little small, but on weekends people get dancing if the band knows what they're doing. ⌂ *prohibition.net; 212-579-3100; 503 Columbus Ave.; Sun-Tues till 2 AM, Wed-Sat till 4 AM.*

Empire Hotel _{Rooftop, Dance Club}

This is quite possibly the only place you'll find high heels and people dancing on the UWS. It's overpriced, the dance floor is tiny, and there's a $20 cover for guys after 11 p.m., but the women are definitely the best you'll get in this part of town. ⌂ *empirehotelnyc.com; 212-956-3313; 44 W 63rd St.; Fri & Sat till 4 AM.*

One Step Beyond _{Themed Bar, Dance Club}

Once a month, the Museum of Natural History converts the Hayden planetarium into the world's oddest nightclub. The music isn't great, the drinks are pricey, and it's more of a nerd convention than a dance party, but it's still kind of cool. ⌂ *amnh.org; 212-769-5200; Central Park West and 81st St.; till 1 AM.*

Above 96th (Around Columbia University)

1020 _{College Bar, Dive Bar, TOP PICK!}

The unofficial campus bar of Columbia University. From Thursday to Saturday when school in is session, it might be the only dive bar in the world where women line up in high heels behind a velvet rope. However, at other times the bar is dead by 2 a.m. Its narrow shape and low table seating isn't ideal, but beers go for $4, there's a pool table, and it's the best of bad lot for picking up Ivy Leaguers. ⌂ *212-531-3468; 1020 Amsterdam Ave. (cnr of 110th).; till 4 AM.*

Amsterdam Tavern _{Pub}

A moderately priced bar that's worth a punt on the weekend. Its layout is a little better for approaching than other bars in the area, and on Sundays it's sometimes the last stop on the nearby hostel's pub crawl. ⌂ *amsterdamtavernnyc.com; 212-280-8070; 938 Amsterdam Ave.; Midweek till quiet, Fri & Sat till 4 AM.*

Bernheim & Schwartz Gastropub, College Bar

This gastropub didn't even register on the map until it recently started hosting 'senior nights' for Columbia students on Wednesdays: probably the best weekly party in the area. There're drink specials, shuffleboard tables, and tons of Ivy League tail. Just get there early because the party is over by 1.30 a.m. ⌂ *bernheimandschwartz.com; 212-335-2911; 2911 Broadway (cnr of 114th); till 1 AM.*

Mel's Burger Bar Gastropub, College Bar

A mediocre restaurant that transforms into a party spot for Columbia students from Thursday to Saturday. It's a lot larger than 1020, but it closes very early. ⌂ *melsburgerbar.com; 212-865-7100; 2850 Broadway; Amsterdam Ave.; till 1 AM.*

Lion's Head Dive Bar, College Bar

This bar is usually a disappointing sausage-fest, but it's often the last resort when 1020 and others are dead or closed. On Wednesdays, it competes with Bernheim & Schwartz with $2 beers, but instead of students you get more locals, young professionals, and "the type that don't tip," as the bartender said (code for tourists and grammatically-challenged minorities). I challenge you to finish their infamous ass-burner wings. ⌂ *lionsheadnyc.com; 212-866-1030; 995 Amsterdam Ave.; till 4 AM.*

The 'dam Dive Bar

Right across the road from both Lion's Head and 1020 is my favorite little hole-in-the-wall on the UWS. It was my local while I lived here, so I feel I have to mention it. It's not a pick-up spot or anything, but it's a place I call home. Jeremy the bartender is a legend, and all beers and well drinks are just $4 after 1 a.m. ⌂ *thedamnyc.com; 212-257-4998; 998 Amsterdam Ave.; till 4 AM.*

Upper East Side (UES)

The Upper East Side is the wealthiest, whitest, and most elderly neighbor in NYC. It's base camp for old money Republicans, 56,000 Jews, and the privileged princesses that inspired the show *Gossip Girl*. It has the most favorable sex ratio in NYC in terms of single females to single males, but a large cohort of these women are 40-something careerists with a penchant for fur coats and purse dogs. As such, the nightlife is so limited it almost makes the Upper West Side look good. As one blogger put it: "There is nightlife on the Upper East Side, and it's called the inside of my eyelids."

However, in recent times the area has become relatively more affordable (presumably for having only one shitty train line that is always ridiculously packed). This change has led to a much-needed injection of young blood. When it comes to women, if you have a preference for light skin, there are few better places than the UES on the weekend.

Most of the action happens on 2nd Avenue, concentrated between 76th and 86th Street. Here there are about a dozen decent bars ranging from cheap college spots to swanky lounges. Start south and get some cheap brews at **The Stumble Inn** and work your way up. If you're into well-heeled, good-looking white girls, the best spot is **The Penrose**. For easy 6s and a small dance floor, there's **Dorrian's**.

North of 96th Street, you're moving into Spanish Harlem (El Barrio), a nightlife dead zone.

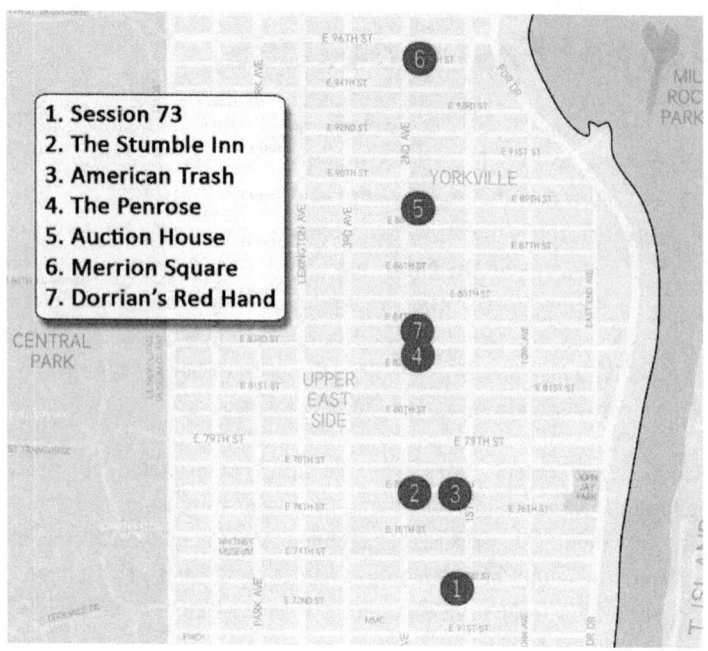

1. Session 73
2. The Stumble Inn
3. American Trash
4. The Penrose
5. Auction House
6. Merrion Square
7. Dorrian's Red Hand

Area Profile

Population: 218k

Average Age: 42, with 26% aged between 20 and 35.

Race: 80% White, 7% Hispanic, 8% Asian, 3% Black, 2% other.

Upper East Side

The Penrose Lounge, Gastropub, TOP PICK!

On weekends this upscale gastropub gets packed with an urbane young crowd. There's plenty of talent on display, and it's a good environment for picking up. If you like white girls, this is the spot. ⌂ *penrosebar.com; 1590 2nd Ave. (Btwn 82nd and 83rd); 212-203-2751; till 4 AM on weekends.*

The Stumble Inn ^{Dive Bar, College Bar}

Yet another NYC Best Bar group franchise offering the typical frat party experience, with cheap drink, beer pong, and hot wings. Monday is dollar beer night. Don't expect to find many women. ○ *nycbestbar.com/stumble; 1454 2nd Ave; 212-650-0561; till 4 AM.*

Auction House ^{Date Spot}

This classy little joint has the feel of a Victorian bordello and is probably the best place for an intimate date in the area. ○ *auctionhousenyc.com; 212-427-4458; 300 E 89th St. (cnr of 2nd Ave); weekdays till quiet, Fri & Sat till 4 AM.*

Session 73 ^{Live Music}

This bar has live music every night, and there's no cover charge. On weekends it attracts a young party crowd. ○ *session73.com; 212-517-4445; 1359 1st Ave. (Btwn 72nd and 73rd); weekdays till 2 AM, Fri & Sat till 4 AM.*

Merrion Square ^{Dive Bar}

If you're stuck up around 96th Street, this place is a good dive option south of El Barrio. There's a pool table, a great beer selection, and you get a free burger with every pint! ○ *merrionnyc.com; 212-831-7696; 1840 2nd Ave; till 4 AM.*

American Trash ^{Dive Bar}

A serious dive. If you want to get wasted on the cheap before hitting up the 2nd Ave., you can also get four mystery shots for $12. ○ *americantrashnyc.com; 929-236-4208; 1471 1st Ave. (Btwn 76th and 77th St.); till 4 AM.*

Dorrian's Red Hand ^{Disco Bar}

After 11 p.m. on weekends, the small back room of this otherwise boring Irish pub becomes a sloppy hook up spot for 6s. ○ *dorrians-nyc.com; 212-772-6660; 1616 2nd Ave; till 4 AM.*

Harlem and Upper Manhattan

Harlem has changed dramatically in recent years. As gentrification creeps north, new bars are slowly popping up in this once sleepy part of town.

The biggest change has happened in West Harlem in my 'hood, Hamilton Heights. In recent years, this predominantly Dominican neighborhood has experienced an invasion of college students, artists, gay men, and young white professionals. Five years ago there were practically no bars in my zip code—but at the time of writing, ~~four~~ five have opened in the last year alone! Most the action in this area is centered on Broadway in the 140's. The most popular bars are **At the Wallace** and neighboring **Harlem Public**. That said, I much prefer the bar scene in Central Harlem.

As you move towards the center on the island, you'll hear Spanish start to be replaced by English and French. Most the population are of African descent, with many from the Caribbean and Francophone West Africa. There are a few good bar options just north of 125th Street on Malcolm X Blvd. Go for a few pints and hit of few hotties at **Corner Social**. You can also nip across the road to sultry cocktail lounge and dance spot **Ginny's Supper Club**. My favorite venue in that area is **The Shrine.** The next nightlife area is on Fredrick Douglas Street north of 110th Street. Here the cultural lines that once separated Harlem from the Upper West Side get a little blurry. My favorite drinking holes are **67 Orange Street** (Harlem's only speakeasy) and West African hangout **Silvana**.

East of Malcolm X Blvd bar options are extremely limited except for a few spots on 116th Street in East Harlem. At the top of the island are the Hispanic neighborhoods of Washington Heights and Inwood. For an adventurous night out, go for a pub crawl on **Dyckman Street** by the A train stop.

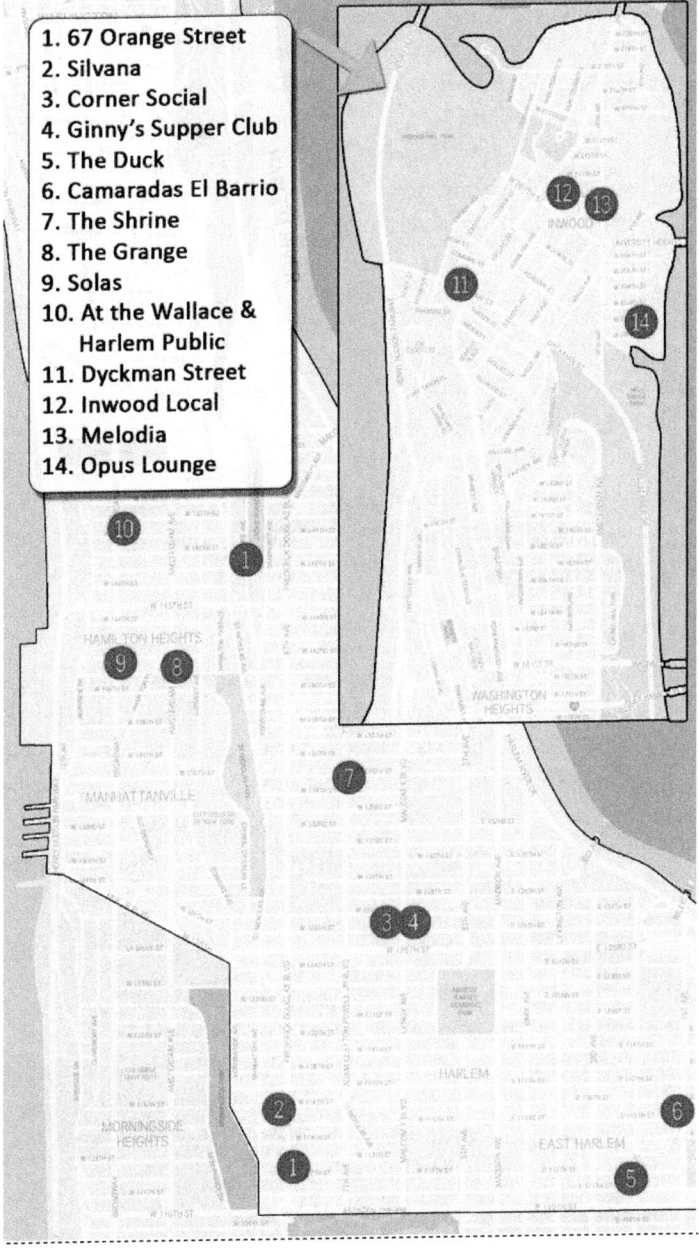

1. 67 Orange Street
2. Silvana
3. Corner Social
4. Ginny's Supper Club
5. The Duck
6. Camaradas El Barrio
7. The Shrine
8. The Grange
9. Solas
10. At the Wallace &
    Harlem Public
11. Dyckman Street
12. Inwood Local
13. Melodia
14. Opus Lounge

Area Profile

Population: 345k in Harlem and 190k in Upper Manhattan.
Average Age: 35 in Harlem and 36 in Washington Heights and
Inwood, with 26% and 28% aged between 20 and 35, respectfully.
Race: 41% Black, 40% Hispanic, 16% White, and 3% other
(Harlem). 72% Hispanic, 16% White, 8% Black, 2% Asian, and
2% other (Washington Heights and Inwood).

West Harlem

Harlem Public American Bar

This little establishment is easily the busiest bar in the area, but it's
a little overrated in my opinion. The seating is very restaurant
orientated, and the bar is small, and the female clientele aren't up
too much, making it a poor place to pick up. ⌂ *harlempublic.com;
3612 Broadway (cnr of 149th); open till 4 AM.*

At the Wallace Dive Bar

Recently opened by the same people from Harlem Public next
door, this spot is more of a dive-bar concept. There's giant Jenga,
shuffleboard, and hot dogs. Things die off here around 2 a.m., and
it's usually a cock-fest, but it's probably the most fun bar in the
area and is a welcome addition. ⌂ *harlempublic.com; 212-234-
6896; 3612 Broadway (cnr of 149th); open weekdays till slow,
weekends till 3.30AM.*

The Grange Bar, Restaurant

This is the last chance saloon in West Harlem for picking up. It's a
little uppity and more of a restaurant, but there's no riff-raff and
it's the only place in the neighborhood that will serve you right up
until 4 a.m. Luckily, the wine bar feel of the place always seems to
attract more girls than guys. ⌂ *thegrangebarnyc.com; 1635
Amsterdam Ave. (cnr of 141st); till 4 AM.*

Solace ^{Latin Bar, Gastropub}

A boxy little Latin bar with a rustic feel, hookahs, and a DJ weekends. It's something different from the other bars in the area. Don't a expect a crowd midweek, but on weekends you can find a few nice Latinas. ⌂ *www.solacebar.com; 3496 Broadway (cnr of 143rd); midweek till 12 AM , Fri & Sat till 4 AM.*

Central Harlem

Corner Social ^{Bar, Lounge}

A large bar with plenty of classy women of a darker shade, as well as some Latinas. On weekends there's a DJ and it's a great place to pick up. The dress code is smart casual. There's also Cove Lounge next door and Ginny's Supper Club across the street. *cornersocialnyc.com; 212-510-8552; 321 Malcolm x Blvd. (Btwn 126th and 127th); weekdays till 2 AM, weekends till 4 AM.*

Ginny's Supper Club ^{Speakeasy, Dance Club, Live Music}

Across the road from Corner Social, you'll find this classy cocktail bar/dance club hid in the basement of Red Rooster. The drinks are expensive, the crowd is a little more mature, and there's usually a cover on weekends, but if you like non-ratchet black ladies this place is a great option. ⌂ *ginnyssupperclub.com; 212-421-3821; 310 Malcolm X Blvd (Btwn 125th and 126th St.); Thurs till 2 AM, Fri & Sat till 3 AM, Sun till 3.30AM.*

Shrine ^{Bar, Music Venue, Dance Club, TOP PICK!}

Modeled after a club in Burkina Faso, this venue is one of my favorite venues in Harlem. It attracts a laid-back mixed crowd and has live music every night. Check their website to see who's playing. After midnight, they clear the tables to make a dance floor that attracts a lot of large 'fluffy' African girls. ⌂ *www.shrinenyc.com; 212-690-7807; 2271 Adam Clayton (cnr of 134th); till 4 AM.*

67 Orange Street Speakeasy, Date Spot

You'd never notice this hidden little cocktail lounge walking by its curtain-covered storefront. Harlem's only speakeasy is pretty standard—a nostalgic feel with bespoke cocktails and suited up bartenders—but instead of jazz there's hip-hop music. They also have their menus hid in children's books. *67orangestreet.com; 212-662-2030; 2082 Fredrick Douglas St. (cnr of 113th); Sun-Tues till 12 AM, Wed-Thurs till 2 AM, Fri & Sat till 4 AM.*

Downstairs at Silvana Live Music, Dance Club, TOP PICK!

Owned by the same people behind Shrine, the small basement of this restaurant hosts Harlem's most unique party. There's hookahs, live music, late night DJs, and the crowd is a mix of Africans and Europeans. There's a house party vibe and dancing is always encouraged (unlike every other venue north of 59th street). It can be hit or miss early in the week, and there's sometimes a cover on weekends, but it's something different and my top pick for letting loose in Harlem (and for picking up African women). ♢ *silvana-nyc.com; 646-692-4935; 300 W 116th St, (cnr of Fredrick Douglas); open weekdays till slow, weekends till 3.30 AM.*

East Harlem (El Barrio)

The Duck Dive Bar

This honky-tonk style dive bar is the best place to drown your sorrows for being north of 96th Street on the east side. ♢ *2171 2nd Ave. (Btwn 111th and 112th); till 4 AM.*

Camaradas El Barrio Live Music, Latin Spot

A narrow Puerto Rican-style pub with a good vibe, live music, and DJs. It ain't much, but it's the best you're going to get in the area. Check online to see what's going on. ♢ *camaradaselbarrio.com; 212-348-2703; 2241 1st Ave. (115th and 116th St.); Sun-Tues till 12 AM, Wed & Thurs till 2 AM, Fri & Sat till 3 AM.*

Washington Heights & Inwood

Dyckman Street ^{Bar Strip}

One the few genuine bar strips in New York City. If you like Latin women, this is probably the best place for a pub crawl. Located north of Broadway right by the A train stop, there are just over half a dozen little Latin spots. The dress code is smart casual. Start at the top and end up in the largest and coolest venue, **Papasitos**. Here you'll find the highest concentration of women and the most people dancing. The police have tried to clamp down on these venues for bravely defying the cabaret laws, but for the moment it's still rocking. ⌂ *Dyckman Street A train stop; till 4 AM.*

Inwood Local ^{American Bar}

Owned by the same people behind Harlem Public. It's a good option if you're looking for a 'normal' bar among all the draft-free Latin bars in the area. There's also a beer garden. ⌂ *212-544-8900; 4957 Broadway (by the 207 stop); till 3 AM.*

Melodia Lounge ^{Dance Club}

A ghetto-fabulous Latin club that's agreeable if like the sound of reggaeton and barely legal Dominicanas. There's free entry before midnight and $10 afterward. The drinks are overpriced, so pregame. ⌂ *718-852-7575; 194 Post Ave.; Thurs-Sat till 4 AM.*

Opus Lounge ^{Latin Spot, Dance Club}

A decent-sized high-end dance club with the sexiest crowd north of Harlem. But be warned: the music is mostly Latin, drinks are pricey, and there's a cover. I'd only recommend a visit if you pregame and speak basic Spanish. ⌂ *opusloungenyc.com; 212-304-0043; 417 W 202nd St; till 4 AM.*

Queens

Queens is the largest of the five boroughs and is said to be the most ethnically diverse place on the planet. 48% of its population are foreign born. I lived here for three months and explored it extensively, but for practical purposes I've excluded everything east of Jackson Heights because it's just too far out from the city center.

For the short-term visitor, I'd honestly recommend you skip Queens—Manhattan and Brooklyn are ten times better—but if you're adamant, Astoria and Woodside have the least shitty options. For those moving here, I've also included info on other neighborhoods.

In Astoria, there are a few hookah lounges and dance spots on the northern end of **Steinway Street** and around the **Astoria-Ditmars** subway stop. On weekends most of these places charge a cover, but they're a few exceptions. The most well-known venues in the part of town are **Bohemian Beer Hall** and **Central** nightclub.

Outside of Astoria options are few and far between. Skipping the ghost town of Long Island City, and moving east along the 7 train, you have the quiet neighborhoods of Sunnyside and Woodside, both of which are half-decent on the weekend. In Sunnyside (my old 'hood), there are several Irish pubs along **Queen's Boulevard**. Molly May's and Gaslight are the best of these for picking up white women and English speakers. You can also find easy C-grade Latina cougars at Arriba Arriba. Woodside has better options, the best of which is the Saturday night scene at **Sean Og's**, with cheap beer, a small dance floor, and tons of Himalayan women.

Farther east there're the Spanish neighborhoods of Jackson Heights and Elmhurst. The nightlife scene there is more lively than in Sunnyside and Woodside, but the majority of the bars are seedy places called 'bailaderos' that cater to Central American male immigrants who pay women to dance with them. That said, there are plenty of sexy women about, and you can pick them up if your game is strong.

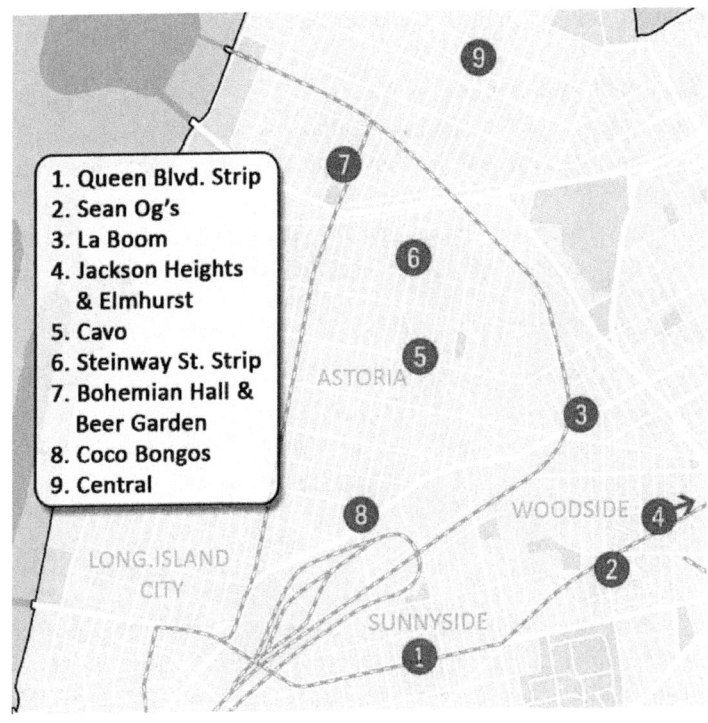

1. Queen Blvd. Strip
2. Sean Og's
3. La Boom
4. Jackson Heights
   & Elmhurst
5. Cavo
6. Steinway St. Strip
7. Bohemian Hall &
   Beer Garden
8. Coco Bongos
9. Central

Area Profile

Population: 2.3 million
Average Age: 39, with 24% aged between 20 and 35.
Race: 28% Hispanic, 26% White, 24% Asian, 17% Black, 5% other.

Astoria

Steinway Street Strip ^{Bar Strip}

From 30th to 23rd Avenue there are several lively drinking spots. Most of these are small Hookahs lounges that somehow have the gall to charge a $10 cover, but that's not always the case. If you don't know a thing about Astoria, this is not a bad area to start. It's certainly better than the boring scene on Broadway.

Bohemian Hall & Beer Garden ^{Beer Hall}

This well-known beer hall is a little overrated in my opinion. It sometimes attracts students, but I'd only recommend it if you happen to be in the area during summer and are in the mood for a stein and sausages. ⌂ *bohemianhall.com; 718-274-4925; 2919 24th Ave.; till Sun-Thurs till 1 AM, Fri & Sat till 3 AM.*

Central ^{Dance Club, Models and Bottles}

A little bit of Meatpacking in Astoria. There's a pretentious vibe and drinks are overpriced, but there's no cover, and the crowd is good-looking. The music is a mix of EDM and Greek. ⌂ *centrallounge.com; 718-726-1600; 20-30 Steinway St; Fri & Sat till 4 AM.*

Coco Bongo ^{Latin Spot, Dance Club}

A decent-sized club that mainly caters to Hispanics. It's $10 in before midnight, but that includes a free drink. There're lots of good-looking women, but like everything else is Astoria, it's overpriced and needlessly pretentious. ⌂ *cocobongony.com; 718-569-7854; 3621 Steinway St.; Fri & Sat till 4 AM.*

Cavo ^{Dance Club}

Just off the Steinway Street bar strip, this restaurant converts into an upscale nightclub on weekends. ⌂ *718-956-7200; 3108 Astoria Blvd; Thurs-Sun till 4 AM.*

Sunnyside & Woodside

La Boom Latin, Dance Club, Live Music

An overpriced, but spacious Latin dance club in Woodside with lots of sexy Latinas. It's usually $30+ for admission and $9 for bottled beers, but if you go to their website, they have 'free admission' tickets on certain nights if you arrive before midnight. Pregame heavily. ⌂ *laboomny.com; 718-726-6646; 56-15 Northern Blvd; Fri-Sun till 4 AM.*

Sean Og's Irish Pub, Disco Bar, TOP PICK!

I don't know how it happened, but for some reason this little Irish pub in Woodside has become the unofficial party headquarters for single Himalayans on Saturday nights. Aside from the sexy Tibetan and Nepalese girls, there's also a good mix of other nationalities—plus there's a dance floor, drink specials, and no cover charge. I've had some great nights out here. ⌂ *718-899-3499; 60-02 Woodside Ave.; till 4 AM.*

The Queens Boulevard Strip

Most of the action in Sunnyside takes place in the Irish pubs along Queens Boulevard. The best of these are **Molly May's** and **Gaslight** (the latter of which is great for after-hours). Both go late and attract the most singles in the area: mainly Irish migrants and white Americans. For Latin girls, Mexican restaurant **Arriba Arriba** turns into a small dance spot after midnight on weekends. I've gotten lucky at all three of these places on numerous occasions. ⌂ *Queens Boulevard at the 40th St. Station on the 7 train; till 4 AM.*

Jackson Heights & Elmhurst

Roosevelt Avenue ^{Bar Strip}

Most of the bars in Jackson Heights are known as 'bailaderos': bizarre disco bars where well-dressed Latinas hustle men into buying dances (at $3-5 a song) and 'lady drinks' for which they receive a commission. The majority of these girls tend to be either Colombian or Dominican, and they ooze sex appeal, whereas most of the male clientele consists of fat little indigenous dudes from Central America. I wouldn't normally recommend such places, but some of the women are top quality, and you can actually pull from them. Without dropping a dime I banged one the sexiest girls I met in the city from one of these places. She told me girls like herself make $300+ a night, so your best bet is to exchange numbers, keep moving, and let her get on with her hustle. It's a seedy scene, but at worst these bars make a very interesting and unique pub crawl. The places to check out are **Mangos**, **Meleo,** and **La Nueva Escuelita.** Another well-known spot is **Hairos**.

Glazz ^{Dance Club, Latin}

Another overpriced mega-club in Queens that's too big not to mention. Expect a mixed crowd, Latin music, and lots of slutty ghetto chicks in high heels. It's usually $20 for guys at the door. It's only worth it if you're stuck in the area and are already buzzed. ⌂ *718-505-1170; 7951 Albion Ave.; Fri & Sat till 4 AM.*

Brooklyn

In my humble opinion, Brooklyn is neck-in-neck with the Lower East Side for having the coolest party scene in New York City. It's unpretentious, eclectic, and always lively. Every time you jump on the L train it's an adventure.

Most of the nightlife is concentrated in Williamsburg, with the Bedford and Lorimer train stops being the main focal points. Nightlife is abundant here, but quite spread out. The party scene is roughly bounded by the Williamsburg Bridge in the south, the East River in the west, and spills north into southern Greenpoint and east of Brooklyn-Queens Expressway. Midweek **The Levee** and neighboring **Skinny Dennis** are good options. On the weekend, your options are almost limitless. If you like rock bars, check out **Rocka Rolla**. If you want to dance, there's **Output** and **Verboten**. For college chicks and tourists there's the infamous meat market **Union Pool**.

Beyond Williamsburg, the only other area worth checking out is the new bohemian bastion of Bushwick. Most of nightlife there can be found between the Jefferson and Morgan Street stations on the L line and the Myrtle Ave. station on the J, Z, and M lines. This area is supposedly what Williamsburg was like a decade ago before it became 'mainstream'. In this part of Bushwick you'll find buildings covered in street art, rock bars, and warehouses converted into cool dance spots. The area is supposedly 'hipster' but the crowd is very diverse. Go on the weekend. Start off with some cheap brews and live music at rock bar **Cobra Club** and end up at **Lot 45** to pick up some raver chicks.

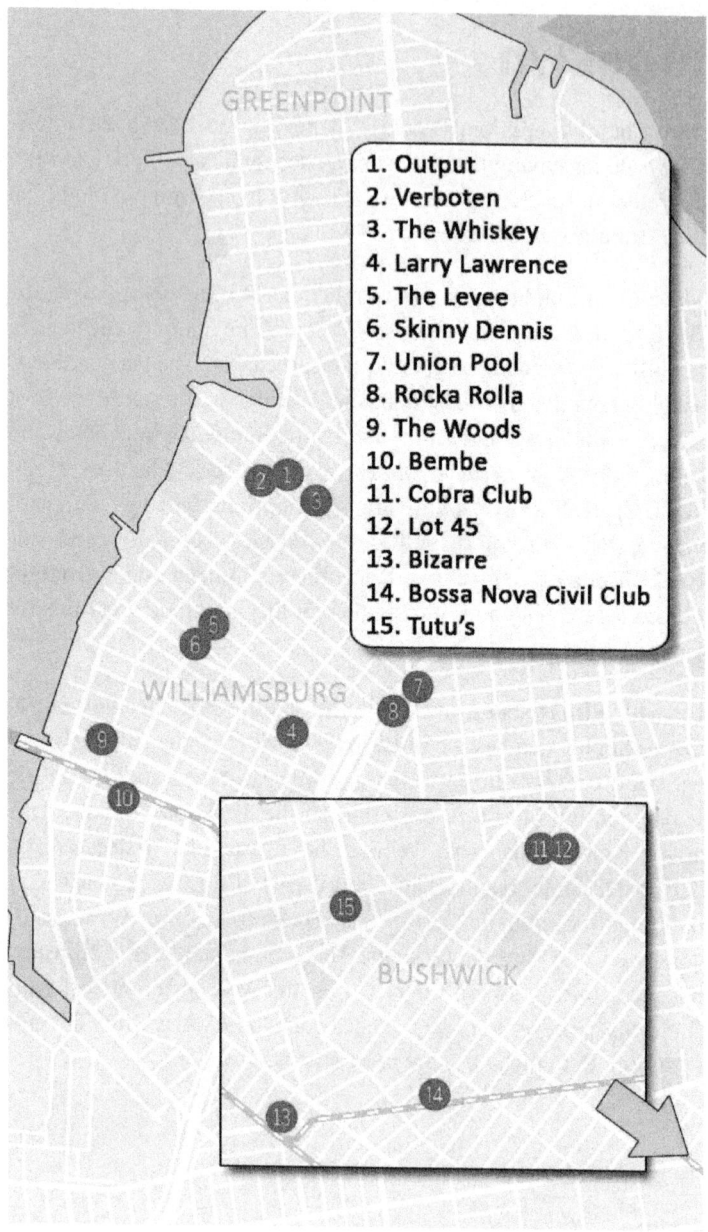

1. Output
2. Verboten
3. The Whiskey
4. Larry Lawrence
5. The Levee
6. Skinny Dennis
7. Union Pool
8. Rocka Rolla
9. The Woods
10. Bembe
11. Cobra Club
12. Lot 45
13. Bizarre
14. Bossa Nova Civil Club
15. Tutu's

GREENPOINT

WILLIAMSBURG

BUSHWICK

Area Profile

Population: 2.6 million total (334k in Williamsburg, Greenpoint, and Bushwick combined)
Average Age: 33, with 16% aged between 20 and 35.
Race: 36% White, 31% Black, 20% Hispanic, 11% Asian, 2% other.

Williamsburg

Rocka Rolla Rock Bar, Dive Bar, TOP PICK!

Finally, a *true* rock bar in Williamsburg. The same crowd behind Skinny Dennis opened this place recently, and they hit the ball out of the park once again. This joint pays homage to a by-gone era with cheap brews, scantily-clad tattooed bartenders, and old-school rock legends like Iron Maiden blasting through the speakers. There's a cool little smoking area, a lively atmosphere, and on weekends it's packed with all sorts. ⌂ *486 Metropolitan Ave.; till 4 AM.*

Skinny Dennis Dive Bar, Live Music, TOP PICK!

A cool honky-tonk saloon with cheap beer, games, and live country music every night. The quality of girls is poor (unless you like white rednecks), but it's consistently busy during the week, a rarity in NYC. I've ended up here countless times and always had a good time. Sunday during the daytime the place is always a riot. ⌂ *skinnydennisbar.com; 212-555-1212; 152 Metropolitan Ave.; till 4 AM.*

The Levee Dive Bar, Rock Bar

Like nearby Skinny Dennis, this hipster/punk horseshoe bar attracts a decent crowd most nights. With a shot and can of beer for only $5, it's one of the cheapest places in the city to catch a buzz. There's also a pool table and board games. ⌂ *theleveenyc.com; 718- 218-8787; 212 Berry Street; till 4 AM.*

Union Pool ^{Disco Bar, Dive Bar}

A notorious meat market with $3 beers, a ton of hipsters, and a taco truck in the back. It's a decent size and known as a hookup spot. The crowd can be very hit or miss, the girls are a little dumpy, and the ratio can be brutal, but when it's good, it's very good. I've lost count of the number of times I've ended up here after Rocka Rolla. ⌂ *union-pool.com; 718-609-0484; 484 Union Ave; till 4 AM.*

Larry Lawrence ^{Speakeasy, Date Spot}

One of the more in-the-know bars in Williamsburg. This dimly-lit little den is the nearest thing to a speakeasy in the area because of the barely marked entrance, but it's a lot more divey than it's Manhattan counterparts. ⌂ *larrylawrencebar.com; 718-218-7866; 295 Grand St.; till 4 AM.*

The Whiskey ^{College Bar, Dive Bar}

It has a bad rep as a 'bro bar', but I still think it's a good choice. Downstairs has a large bar with a DJ, shuffleboard tables, and arcade games. It feels more like a college bar than the typical 'cooler' spots in the area, but there's a lot of options for picking up and a good party atmosphere. ⌂ *whiskeybrooklyn.com; 718-387-8444; 44 Berry Street; till 4 AM.*

Output ^{Dance Club, Rooftop}

The most famous dance club in Brooklyn. This unpretentious warehouse club has multiple levels, a rooftop, and no door policy. That said, it's pretty dark, feels quite industrial, and blasts nothing but EDM all night. To quote their website: "Output is open to anyone, but is not for everyone." Entry varies from free to $20 depending on the night. ⌂ *outputclub.com; 74 Wythe Ave.; Wed-Sun till 4 AM.*

Verboten Bar Dance Club

Another warehouse club from by the same people behind Output around the corner. It's similar to its older brother, but it's half the size, more expensive, and has a stricter door (a good thing for women). Expect to pay a $20-30 cover. The one big selling point about this place is that it goes till 6 a.m. on weekends. ⌂ *verbotennewyork.com; 347-223-4732; 54 N 11th St; Wed, Thurs & Sun till 4 AM, Fri & Sat till 6 AM.*

Bembe Disco Bar, Live Music

A tiny venue with a big reputation. The island vibe music attracts a diverse crowd. It's not a bad alternative to The Woods nearby, but in my opinion it's too pokey to warrant the $10 cover on weekends. Reggae night on Tuesdays in very popular. I also like the bands on Wednesday nights, but it's not very well attended. ⌂ *bembe.us; 718-387-5389; 81 S 6th St.; till 4 AM.*

The Woods Disco Bar

A well-known disco bar that packs up on weekends. The crowd is a mix of hipster chic and bridge and tunnel posers. It's a bit out of the way and there's a $10 cover for guys, but it's not a bad option if you want something less intense than Output, but a step up from Union Pool. If you're not feeling it here, there's also TBD and Bembe nearby. ⌂ *thewoodsbk.com; 718-782-4955; 48 S 4th St.; till 4 AM.*

Bushwick

The Cobra Club Rock Bar, Dive Bar

A badass biker bar just off the Jefferson St. stop. The place has a grungy vibe, a mixed crowd, and a back room with live music. It's not a bad place to pick up or pregame. You can get a beer and shot for $6. ⌂ *cobraclubbk.com; 917-719-1138; 6 Wyckoff Ave.; Sun-Thurs till AM, Fri & Sat till 4 AM.*

Bossa Nova Civil Club Bar, Dance Club

A popular dance venue with reasonably priced drinks, good vibes, and a cool crowd. Expect fog machines and techno. There's a $10 cover on weekends. △ *bossanovacivicclub.com; 718-443-1271; 1271 Myrtle Ave.; till 4 AM.*

Tutu's Disco Bar

On the weekend, the back room of this place converts into a cool little dance area. This spot is a pick up favorite for local Lothario Goldmund (from goldmununleashed.com). △ *tutusbrooklyn.com; 718- 456-7898; 25 Bogart St.; till 4 AM.*

Bizarre Themed Bar

A large bar that lives up to its name, doubling as a performance space for edgy acts that often involve nudity. It's worth a visit on a Bushwick pub crawl. △ *bizarrebushwick.com; 347-915-2717; 12 Jefferson St; till 4 AM.*

Lot 45 Lounge, Dance Club, TOP PICK!

A huge warehouse that was converted into a dance lounge. This is one the coolest spaces in the city. The crowd is a diverse bunch, and the women are the best I've seen in Bushwick, too. That said, I think it tries to be a little 'too cool for school'. My first experience was poor. The music was some dreadful minimalist electro crap, and it took me twenty minutes to get served. Still, I recommend that you check it out. △ *lot45bushwick.com; 347-505-9155; 411 Troutman St; Tues-Thurs till 2 AM, Fri & Sat till 4 AM.*

ABOUT THE AUTHOR

Mark Zolo was born in Dublin, Ireland. He has traveled to over 90 countries, as well as Antarctica and several self-proclaimed republics.

He is the author of the Amazon no.1 travel memoir *Naughty Nomad: Not your typical backpacker story*. Google it. The reviews online speak for themselves.

He is also known for traveling to war zones with a crew of Mexican pirates (seriously). You can catch his antics by watching the YouTube mini-series *The Way to Mogadishu,* filmed in Somalia.

You can also follow his adventures on his website, naughtynomad.com, and become part of the Naughty Nomad community by signing up at naughtynomadforum.com.

Mark is currently working on his second travel memoir detailing his experiences as a swashbuckling playboy in West Africa, the Middle East, and other exotic destinations.

Printed in Great Britain
by Amazon

58211983R00079